contents

Parent-Training Programmes for the Management of Young Children with Conduct Disorders: Findings from Research

JOANNA RICHARDSON & CAROL JOUGHIN

© The Royal College of Psychiatrists 2002.

Gaskell is an imprint of the Royal College of Psychiatrists, 17 Belgrave Square, London SW1X 8PG. All rights reserved. No part of this book may be reprinted or reproduced or utilised in any form or by any electronic, mechanical or other means, now known or hereafter invented, including photocopying and recording, or in any information storage or retrieval system, without permission in writing from the publishers.

British Library Cataloguing-in-Publication Data
A catalogue record for this book is available from the British Library.
ISBN 1-901242-80-3

The views presented in this book do not necessarily reflect those of the Royal College of Psychiatrists, and the publishers are not responsible for any error of omission or fact.

Gaskell is a registered trademark of the Royal College of Psychiatrists.
The Royal College of Psychiatrists is a registered charity (no. 228636).

Cover illustration by Michèlle Skelton. Cover design © The Royal College of Psychiatrists 2002.

Printed in Great Britain by Cromwell Press Ltd, Trowbridge, UK.

preface

The appropriate management of children with conduct disorders is an important public health issue that has significant financial implications for health, education and social services. Conduct disorders are the most common form of problem referred to child and adolescent mental health services (Reid, 1993). Parent-training programmes have been shown to be the most effective treatment strategy for children with conduct disorders under 10 years of age (NHS Centre for Reviews and Dissemination, 1997; Brestan & Eyberg, 1998; Barlow, 1999). This report provides an overview of the definitions, epidemiology, long-term outcomes, risk factors and assessment of conduct disorders. The main aim is to present a summary of the key research relating to the use of parent-training programmes for the treatment and prevention of conduct disorders in young children. The report highlights areas that have been shown to improve the efficacy of current initiatives. New research is also presented and critically appraised. In addition, the current provision of parent-training programmes in the UK is discussed.

It is hoped that this report will assist clinicians, managers and commissioners and all other professionals involved in the management of young children with conduct disorders.

acknowledgements

FOCUS would like to thank Professor Stuart Logan from the Institute of Child Health, London, for his advice on how to present the results from the research papers in this report. We would also like to express our thanks to Angela Scott, the Information Services Department at the Royal College of Psychiatrists and the Library at the Institute of Child Health for all the help with obtaining papers for this report.

FOCUS is a strategic dissemination project which aims to promote effective practice in child and adolescent mental health services. FOCUS is funded by the Gatsby Charitable Foundation and the Department of Health (Section 64 grant award).

one conduct disorders: an overview

Key messages

- Conduct disorders are the most common reason for referral of young children to mental health services.
- The prevalence of conduct disorders in 5–10-year-olds is 6.5% for boys and 2.7% for girls.
- Sixty-two per cent of three-year-olds with conduct disorders were found to continue these problems through to the age of eight.
- Children who become violent as adolescents can be identified with almost 50% reliability as early as age seven.
- Approximately 40–50% of children with conduct disorders may develop antisocial personality disorder as adults.
- The estimated annual cost per child if conduct disorder is left untreated is £15,270.
- Five aspects of parenting which have been repeatedly found to have a long-term association with antisocial behaviour are: poor supervision, erratic harsh discipline, parental disharmony, rejection of the child, and low parental involvement in the child's activities.

DEFINITIONS AND TERMINOLOGY

The term 'conduct disorder' is generally used to describe a pattern of repeated and persistent misbehaviour. This misbehaviour is much worse than would normally be expected in a child of that age. The essential feature is a persistent pattern of conduct in which the basic rights of others and major age-appropriate societal norms and rules are violated (American Psychiatric Association, 2000).

Professionals and researchers use a variety of terms to describe conduct disorders. These include disobedient, aggressive, antisocial, challenging behaviour, oppositional, defiant, delinquent and conduct problems. For the purposes of this report we have chosen to use the term 'conduct disorders' to cover children who are described as having either conduct disorder (CD) or, as is more frequently the case in young children, oppositional defiant disorder (ODD). For the full ICD–10 and DSM–IV classifications for CD and ODD see Appendix 1.

Obviously there are a frequency and a severity of certain disruptive behaviours which are expected in young children and are considered part of 'normal' development, and children will usually grow out of them. These behaviours occur as part of the child's developmental process; although they may be difficult for the parents to deal with, they will not be discussed in this report. A number of programmes are provided by various voluntary organisations to address less severe behaviour problems (Smith, 1996).

PREVALENCE

Epidemiological studies suggest that approximately half of those who meet diagnostic mental health criteria for CD will also meet criteria for at least one other disorder. The most frequent combination of problems is hyperactivity with CD, found in about 45–70% of those with CD.

The prevalence of CD in children between the ages of 5 and 10 years is 1.7% for boys and 0.6% for girls (Meltzer *et al*, 2000). Meltzer *et al* (2000) found the prevalence of ODD in 5–10-year-olds to be 4.8% for boys and 2.1% for girls. Although symptoms are generally similar in each gender, boys may have more confrontational behaviour and more persistent symptoms. There are also differences regarding gender in relation to the age of onset of conduct disorders. Robins (1966) found that the median age of onset for children referred to mental health clinics with antisocial behaviour was in the 8–10-year age range. Fifty-seven per cent of boys had an onset before the age of 10 years, whereas for girls the onset was mainly between 14 and 16 years of age.

LONG-TERM OUTCOMES

Conduct disorders have been described as being either those which start in young children and become persistent for the life course or those which emerge in adolescence. Research has shown that there is a particularly poor prognosis attached to early onset, which indicates that early treatments in these groups are essential (Moffit *et al*, 1996). Early starting patterns of conduct disorder are remarkably stable (Farrington, 1989). Richman *et al* (1982) found that 62% of 3-year-olds with conduct disorders continued these problems through to the age of 8. Almost half of all youths who initiated serious violent acts before the age of 11 continued this type of offending beyond the age of 20, twice the rate of those who began their violent careers at age 11 or 12 (Elliott, 1994).

A number of theorists have suggested there should be strong links between disruptive and externalising behaviours in pre-school years and externalising behaviours in adolescents (Rutter, 1985; Loeber, 1990). The hypothesised early-onset pathway begins with the emergence of ODD in early pre-school years and school years and progresses to both aggressive and non-aggressive symptoms (e.g. lying and stealing) of conduct disorders in middle childhood and then to the most serious symptoms by adolescence.

The Isle of Wight study showed that children with conduct disorders at ages 10 and 11 fared worse at follow-up at ages 14 and 15 than children with other problems (Graham & Rutter, 1973). Farrington (1989, 1990), in the Cambridge Study in Delinquent Development, found half of the most antisocial boys at ages 8–10 were still antisocial at age 14 and 43% were still among the most antisocial at age 18. The Conduct Problems Prevention Research Group (1999a), which consists of a group of American researchers involved in the Fast Track project (described in more detail in Chapter 5), argues that although there will be false positives, the probability of identifying the majority of those children who are at serious long-term risk at school entry is high.

Loeber *et al* (1993) demonstrated that children who became violent as adolescents could be identified with almost 50% reliability as early as age 7, as a result of their aggressive and disruptive behaviour at home and at school. Robins (1966, 1978) noted that it was rare to find an antisocial adult who had not exhibited conduct disorders as a child, even though no more than half of the children identified as having conduct disorders go on to become antisocial adults. Studies have shown that approximately 40–50% of children with conduct disorder go on to develop antisocial personality disorder as adults (Robins, 1966; Loeber, 1982; Rutter & Giller, 1983; American Academy of Child and Adolescent Psychiatry, 1997). Children with conduct disorders who do not go on to develop antisocial personality disorder may develop a range of other psychiatric disturbances, including substance misuse, mania, schizophrenia, obsessive–compulsive disorder, major depressive disorder and panic disorder (Robins, 1966; Maughan & Rutter, 1998). Higher rates of violent death have been shown to occur in young people diagnosed with conduct disorder (Rydelius, 1988). Farrington (1995) found that, as well as developing psychiatric problems, many children with conduct disorder develop non-psychiatric antisocial behaviours, which include theft, violence to people and property, drunk driving, use of illegal drugs, carrying and using weapons, and group violence.

Conduct disorders in childhood have also been linked to: failure to complete schooling; joblessness and consequent financial dependency; poor interpersonal relationships, particularly family break-up and divorce. They have also been shown to lead to abuse of the next generation of children, thus increasing the chance of them developing conduct disorders (Rutter & Giller, 1983; Robins, 1991).

Robins (1991) states, 'because conduct disorder is common and has pervasive long-range effects, it is a very important public health problem'.

COST OF TREATING CHILDREN

The cost of conduct disorders, both in terms of the quality of life of those who have conduct disorders (and the people around them) and in terms of the resources necessary to counteract them, is high. It is therefore important that treatment for conduct disorders is both effective and cost-effective.

Knapp et al (1999) state that the NHS resources spent on children with conduct disorders are considerable. Thirty per cent of child consultations with general practitioners are for conduct disorders. Forty-five per cent of community child health referrals are for behaviour disturbances, with an even higher level at schools for children with special needs and in clinics for children with developmental delay, where challenging behaviour is a common problem. Psychiatric disorders are present in 28% of paediatric out-patient referrals.

Social services departments expend a lot of energy trying to protect disruptive children whose parents can no longer cope without hitting or abusing them. Often this may include a brief time with a foster family or the placement of the child in residential care.

Education costs include funding special schools for emotionally and behaviourally disturbed children, as well as providing extra staff to support and provide special-needs education. Law enforcement agencies and the probation service have to detect and prevent delinquency and bring the delinquents to justice. The rate of unemployment and receipt of state benefits is also high among young people with conduct disorders (Rutter et al, 1998).

All agencies will spend considerable amounts of money in supporting a child or young person with conduct disorder over the life span if nothing is done to treat the child. Knapp et al (1999)

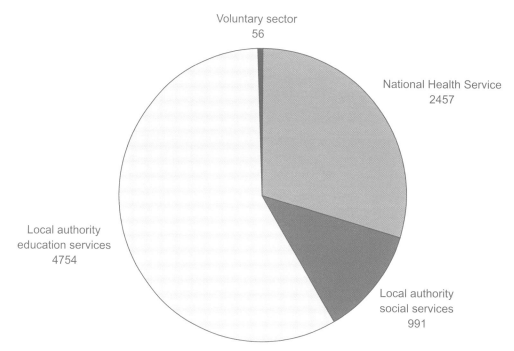

Fig. 1. Annual costs (£) per child with conduct disorder.
Data from paper by Knapp et al (1999), based on a sample of 10 children.

examined the cost of treating children diagnosed with conduct disorder. The total direct costs for all agencies (see Fig. 1 for a breakdown) were £8258. The indirect costs, which included loss of employment for some parents, additional housework and repairs, and allowances and benefits, were estimated to be £7012. The total cost annually per child with conduct disorder was likely to amount therefore to a staggering £15,270.

The House of Commons Health Committee (1997), in its report on child and adolescent mental health services, cited two recent outcome studies of projects in the US aimed at improving the behaviour of children from disadvantaged backgrounds. The two studies also looked at the costs saved by early intervention for conduct disorders.

- The Perry Pre-school Project worked with 3–4-year-olds and looked at real-life outcomes to 19 years of age. This study found fewer delinquent acts, less use of special education and better peer relationships. Compared with controls, there were savings of $14,819 per child (Barnett, 1993; Schweinhart & Weikart, 1997).

- The Yale Project ran a family support programme in the pre-school years and found that at the age of 13 years the children involved got better grades, attended school more regularly and had fewer behaviour problems. Compared with controls, there were savings of $20,000 per family in community resources expended (Seitz et al, 1985).

A consultation document for the National Assembly for Wales (2000) explains that if the NHS were successfully to treat a child with conduct disorder, with an expensive investment in childhood, this would not only save the NHS money over the person's lifetime, but also other public sector organisations could save significant amounts of money in the long run. This approach emphasises the importance of multi-agency working.

RISK FACTORS

Conduct disorders present a significant public health problem for both the individual and the economy. To reduce the frequency of conduct disorders, the first step is to recognise the risk factors for them. These may in turn suggest the causes of conduct disorders and help to identify the children most likely to develop them. Risk factors for the development of conduct disorders may be considered in terms of child, parenting and environmental factors. The interaction of these factors is outlined in Fig. 2.

Child factors

Temperament

Temperament refers to a number of characteristics that show some consistency over time (Normand et al, 1996). These characteristics appear soon after birth (Coffman et al, 1992). A number of studies suggest that infants assessed as having a difficult temperament are more likely to show problems with behaviour later on (Greenberg & Speltz, 1993; Prior et al, 1993). A difficult temperament may make children more likely to be the target of parental anger, which in turn may be linked to conduct disorders later on (Marshall & Watt, 1999). However, Wooton et al (1997) demonstrated a possible strong relationship between 'callous-unemotional' temperament and behaviour problems despite good parenting practices. The authors concluded that these children, with a lack of empathy, lack of guilt and emotional constrictedness, develop conduct disorders through causal factors distinct from other children with conduct disorders.

Genetic

Conduct disorder is thought to differ from attention-deficit hyperactivity disorder (ADHD) in terms of genetic influence. For children with ADHD, the magnitude of the genetic influences is thought to be 60–90% (Goodman & Stevenson, 1989; Thapar et al, 1995; Silberg et al, 1996). There is, however, little evidence to suggest that genetic factors alone contribute to conduct disorder. Plomin (1994) found genetic factors accounted for half the variation of externalising behaviour. Genetic factors plus adverse environmental factors accounted for more of the variation in children with conduct disorders (Eaves et al, 1997). As Walters (1992) states, it is very unlikely that a single gene or even a simple genetic model can account for complex behaviours such as conduct disorders or criminal activity.

Physical illnesses

Rutter et al (1970) found that children with epilepsy or other disorders of cerebral function are at increased risk for conduct as well as emotional disorders. Rutter (1988) found that chronically ill children have three times the incidence of conduct disorders than their peers; if the chronic condition was found to affect the central nervous system (CNS), the risk factor rose approximately fivefold. It has also been shown that perinatal complications such as long labour, delivery with instruments and asphyxia predict conduct disorders and delinquency, although the effects of these complications may vary with other risk factors (Mednick & Kandel, 1988; Raine et al, 1994).

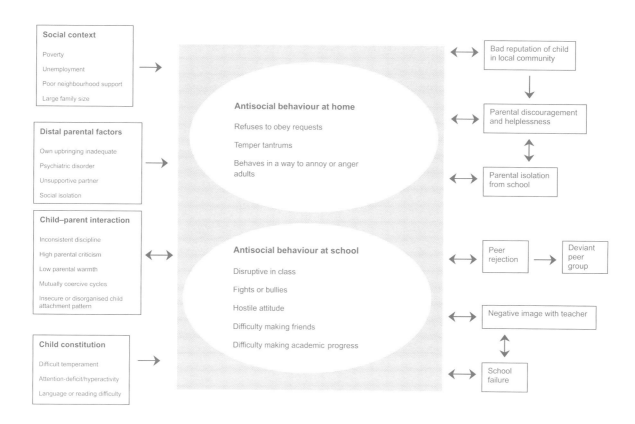

Fig. 2. Influences on antisocial behaviour seen at home and at school, and how the consequences may perpetuate it. (From Spender & Scott, 1997.)

Cognitive deficits

A number of studies have examined the cognitive correlates of conduct disorders in younger children and have found that they often have delays in language development and cognitive functioning (Cantwell & Baker, 1991; Hinshaw, 1992). Language problems, however, could also be considered not to be a child factor, as many factors associated with language development involve the parents' and the child's environment. An example of this is a study which found mother–child interactions and the home environment to be good predictors of language skill by the age of three years (Bee *et al*, 1982).

Cognitive deficits do lead to school underachievement and this has been found to be associated with conduct disorder. Rutter *et al* (1970, 1976) in the Isle of Wight study of 10–11-year-olds found that a third of children with severely delayed reading levels had conduct disorder and a third of children with conduct disorder were severely behind in their reading. Scott (1995) emphasises the importance of turning around educational underachievement in conduct-disordered children due to cognitive deficits, as this leads to a continuing feeling of low self-esteem in the child. This low self-esteem and belief that they are bad (when often the appropriate assessments are not made and so specific reading and learning disabilities may easily be missed) can cause marked misery and unhappiness and, as a result, a higher incidence of depression (Scott, 1995). It has been suggested that academic failure is a cause rather than a consequence of antisocial behaviour; however, programmes that have improved the academic skills of these children have not achieved reductions in antisocial behaviours (Wilson & Herrnstein, 1985). Similar results have been found for peer rejection, despite these children having been given social skills training (Kazdin, 1987).

Poor social skills

Some of these children lack the social skills to maintain friendships and may become isolated from peer groups (Kazdin, 1995). Children engaging in problem behaviours are thought to have underlying distortions or deficits in their social information processing system (Dodge & Schwartz, 1997). Dodge & Price (1994) found that aggressive children were more likely to interpret social cues as provocative and to respond more aggressively to neutral situations. Children who are aggressive or antisocial are often rejected by their peers (Marshall & Watt, 1999). As Dishion *et al* (1991) show, peer group rejection is often a prelude to deviant peer group membership, which reinforces deviant behaviours. It has also been found that aggressive, antisocial children are socially inept in their interactions with adults. They are less likely to defer to adult authority, show politeness and to respond in such ways as to promote further interactions (Freedman *et al*, 1978).

Parenting factors

According to Carr (1999), neglect, abuse, separations, lack of opportunities to develop secure attachments, and harsh, lax or inconsistent discipline are among the more important aspects of the parent–child relationship that place youngsters at risk of developing conduct disorders. Parenting behaviour and parent characteristics such as depression are among the strongest predictors of child behaviour problems (Marshall & Watt, 1999).

Poor parenting skills

Scott (1998) showed that five aspects of how parents bring up their children have been found repeatedly to have a long-term association with conduct disorders. These are:

- poor supervision;
- erratic harsh discipline;
- parental disharmony;
- rejection of the child;
- low parental involvement in the child's activities.

Such parenting appears to be a major cause of conduct disorders in children.

Webster-Stratton & Spitzer (1991) found parents of children with conduct disorders lack fundamental parenting skills and exhibit fewer positive behaviours. Their discipline involves more violence and criticism, and they are more permissive, erratic and inconsistent, and more likely to fail to monitor their child's behaviour, to reinforce inappropriate behaviours and to ignore or punish pro-social behaviours.

Patterson's work shows that parents of antisocial children are deficient in their child-rearing skills (Patterson, 1982; Patterson *et al*, 1989):

- they do not tell their children how they expect them to behave;

- they fail to monitor the behaviour of their children to ensure it is desirable;

- they fail to enforce rules promptly and clearly with positive and negative reinforcement.

Attachment

According to the attachment model proposed by Bowlby (1969), parental responsiveness is conceptualised as critical to the development of self-regulation skills. Therefore, differences in caregiver sensitivity and the resultant bond between the parent and infant are important factors in later patterns of the child's behaviour (Lyons-Ruth, 1996). Greenberg & Speltz (1988) found that children who had received insufficient caregiving will act more disruptively to obtain the attention of their parent. They have less to lose in terms of love (Shaw & Winslow, 1997). Shaw & Winslow (1997) examined infant attachment security and observed the responsiveness of caregivers, and found that the parent–infant relationship correlated with externalising behaviour at a later age.

Poor interactions between mother and child can influence the child in many ways (Marshall & Watt, 1999): the mother's inappropriate modelling of interactional behaviour (Bandura, 1986); the child's development of unrealistic goals and lack of knowledge of social rules within relationships with adults and peers (Goodman & Brumley, 1990); the establishment of coercive patterns of interaction within the parent–child relationship that are carried forward to the peer group (Patterson, 1986); and the impact of a lack of warmth on the child's self-concept (Patterson *et al*, 1989).

Separation and disruption of primary attachments through neglect or abuse may also prevent children from developing internal working models for secure attachments.

Mental health problems in parents

Offord *et al* (1989), in their longitudinal study of single- and two-parent families, found that mothers with psychological distress, major depression or alcohol problems were more than twice as likely to have children with externalising problems directed at others. Stein *et al* (1991) and Beck (1998) found that children older than one year whose mother is postnatally depressed display problems such as insecure attachment, antisocial behaviour and cognitive deficits. Depressed mothers are highly critical of their children, find it difficult to set limits and are often emotionally unavailable. Hall *et al* (1991) report that mothers who are depressed are more likely to perceive their child's behaviour as inappropriate or maladjusted.

West & Farrington (1973) report strong links between the presence of an antisocial personality in one or both parents and similar behaviour in the child.

Substance misuse and criminality in parents

Children coming from families where parents are involved in substance misuse or criminal activities are at particular risk of developing conduct disorders (Patterson *et al*, 1989; Frick *et al*, 1991).

Research has shown that when both parents are alcoholics this increases the chances of children developing ODD and CD (Earls *et al*, 1988). A number of researchers suggest that a combination of risk factors play a role in increasing behaviour problems. Miller & Jang (1977) found that children of alcoholics tend to come from lower-class homes with other problems, including parental mental illness, criminal activity, more marital breakdowns and more welfare assistance. Parents involved in crime may provide deviant role models for children to imitate and substance misuse may compromise parents' capacity to care for their children correctly (Carr, 1999).

Teenage parents

Marshall & Watt (1999) highlight the research showing that children of teenage mothers had more conduct disorders at age 8, 10, and 12 years compared with older mothers. However, as the research goes on to point out, the effects of teenage pregnancy may be due to the fact that children with teenage mothers tend to live on lower incomes, have absent biological fathers and suffer from poor child-rearing practices. Fergusson & Lynskey (1995) found maternal age, socio-economic status, number of siblings at the time of the child's birth and punitive parenting practices were all significant in the relationship between maternal age and conduct disorders.

Marital discord

Marital problems, as previously mentioned, are a risk factor. Marital conflict leading to divorce can have detrimental effects on children (Marshall & Watt, 1999). Marital disruption is often associated with a change in economic circumstances and adjustments to altered living conditions; parents may be distressed and this may affect their parenting practices. Also, separated parents may not agree on rules and how they should be implemented. This may lead to a lack of communication about discipline and in turn to inconsistent disciplinary practices.

Some research suggests that when there is persistent conflict in families in which the parents do not separate, there are high levels of child behaviour problems and poor self-esteem in children (Marshall & Watt, 1999). In a recent study, negative marital conflict management skills on the part of parents (defined as the inability to collaborate and problem solve, to communicate positively about problems and to regulate negative affect) were a key variable in contributing to child conduct disorders (Webster-Stratton & Hammond, 1999).

Marital violence

Marshall & Watt (1999) also provide evidence that marital conflict involving physical aggression is more upsetting to children than other forms of marital conflict. Children exposed to marital violence may imitate this in their relationships with others and display violent behaviour towards family, peers and teachers. Carr (1999) goes on to suggest that where children are exposed to negative emotions, their safety and security may be threatened and therefore they may express anger towards their parents.

Abuse

Abusive and injurious parenting practices are regarded as the most influential risk factors for conduct disorders (Luntz & Widom, 1994). Physically maltreated children were found to be commonly aggressive, non-compliant, to use acting-out behaviour and to perform badly on cognitive tasks. Sexually abused children had a variety of problems, including aggression and withdrawal, and were not liked by their peers (Erickson *et al*, 1989). Child maltreatment is a highly specific risk factor (Finkelhor & Berliner, 1995).

Single parents

Where parents are living alone, they may find the constant pressure of looking after a child, along with domestic and work-related issues, difficult to manage, which can result in inconsistent discipline due to emotional exhaustion and lack of social support networks to help with the children. Parents of children with conduct disorder report major stressors two to four times more often than parents of children without conduct disorder (Webster-Stratton, 1990*a*).

Environmental factors

Social disadvantage, homelessness, low socio-economic status, poverty, overcrowding and social isolation are broader factors that predispose children to conduct disorder (Hausman & Hammen, 1993; American Academy of Child and Adolescent Psychiatry, 1997; Carr, 1999). It seems that the longer the child has been living in poverty within the first four years of life, the more prevalent externalising behaviour problems become (Duncan *et al*, 1994). According to Graham (1991), children from large families and those living in homes where divorce or separation has occurred are at greater risk of conduct disorders. Children with conduct disorders are more likely to come from troubled neighbourhoods. Urban areas have higher rates of conduct disorders; Rutter *et al* (1975) found that conduct disorder was twice as high in inner London than on the Isle of Wight.

It becomes apparent that conduct disorders are extremely complex and pervasive. There are a number of risk factors for conduct disorders, and these can occur in combination. Apart from the direct link between poverty, socio-economic status and child behaviour problems, other factors, which include maternal depression, exposure to violence and poor parenting practices, seem to act as mediators to additional factors (Loeber & Dishion, 1983; Yoshikawa, 1994).

Resilience: protective factors for conduct disorders

Some children appear to have a number of risk factors associated with an increased risk of developing behavioural problems and yet do not go on to have conduct disorders. Rutter (1985) highlighted the importance of vulnerability and protective factors that modulate responses to stress. Werner's (1992, 1994) longitudinal study investigated resilience in over 200 babies born in 1955 on a Hawaiian island, following and assessing the children at various times up to the age of 32 years. Werner found that the resilient children – those with the ability to cope with the internal stresses of their vulnerabilities and the external stresses of their environment – were similar in that they:

• had the ability to elicit positive responses from others and the skills and values that led to an efficient use of their abilities;

• were engaging to other people;

• had good communication and problem-solving skills;

• were able to respond and relate to substitute caregivers;

• had a high IQ, had good abilities and good dispositions;

- had a hobby valued by their peers or elders;

- grew up with five children or less, with at least two years between the child and the next sibling,

- had parents with caregiving skills that led to competence and increased self-esteem.

Pro-social peers and a school that creates success, responsibility and self-discipline have also been shown to be important in preventing behaviour problems (Rutter, 1979).

ASSESSMENT

According to the American Academy of Child and Adolescent Psychiatry (1997), assessment requires the collection of data from a number of informants in multiple settings using multiple methods.

The assessment process is very important and other conditions (such as hyperkinetic disorder) need to be ruled out *before* a diagnosis of CD or ODD is made (see Appendix 1 for ICD–10 criteria). There are a number of assessment tools used to diagnose children with conduct disorders. Some of the most commonly used assessment tools are:

- the Child Behavior Checklist (Achenbach & Edelbrock, 1991),

- the Eyberg Child Behaviour Inventory (Eyberg, 1992),

- the Conners' Parent–Teacher Rating Scales (Conners, 1989; Conners *et al*, 1998*a,b*).

TREATMENT

It has been shown that parent-training programmes are most effective for young children (under 10) with conduct disorders (Bank *et al*, 1991; Kazdin, 1995). This type of intervention is examined in greater detail throughout the rest of the report.

Most services will use the general principles in their practice if not specific parenting programmes. Chapter 7 presents the results of a survey which aimed to ascertain where parent-training pro-grammes are available around the UK and whether current services vary from region to region.

The other main treatments offered to young children with conduct disorders include:

- behavioural therapy;

- psychotherapy;

- family therapy;

- cognitive therapy;

- medication.

the research evidence

Key messages

- The ideal study design to examine the effectiveness of an intervention is a randomised controlled trial with long-term follow-up.
- To assess the quality of research studies the papers need to be critically appraised.
- To be able to interpret the results of a randomised controlled trial or a meta-analysis it is important to understand the meaning of effect size and *P* values.

IDENTIFYING THE RESEARCH EVIDENCE

To identify papers in this area of interest, searches were conducted in July 2000 on the Medline, Psychlit, Embase and Cochrane databases for papers published between 1990 and July 2000. The first search used the term 'ADHD and disruptive behaviour disorders'. This heading included the terms 'oppositional defiant disorder' and 'conduct disorder'. The second term used was 'behavioural problems'. Both terms were searched using filters for randomised controlled trials and systematic reviews and meta-analyses (see Appendix 2 for search strategies used).

For studies to be included in this report the following criteria were applied:

- the majority of children in an individual study had to be under the age of 10 years and to have conduct disorders, or be at a high risk of these disorders;

- where possible the children in the studies would have been assessed and diagnosed with ODD or CD;

- the intervention had to involve some form of parent-training;

- the studies were all in English.

Studies were excluded if:

- the majority of children in a study had learning difficulties or ADHD;

- the intervention did not include parent-training;

- the aim of the programme was to tackle child abuse.

The use of such strict inclusion and exclusion criteria meant that a number of studies that did not specify diagnostic criteria for the recruitment of subjects may have been missed.

Two systematic reviews were identified and appraised. Four randomised controlled trials that were either not included in the systematic reviews or were published after the systematic reviews came out have been critically appraised. Four further randomised controlled trials examining the issue of prevention have also been critically appraised. A summary table of the papers that were selected and appraised in the report can be found in Appendix 3. Summary appraisals of the papers can be also be found in Appendix 3. Critical appraisals of the primary and secondary papers were undertaken using tools adapted from materials produced by the Centre of Evidence-Based Mental Health. The tables of the appraised individual papers that were included in Barlow's (1999) systematic review can be found in Appendix 4.

Readers are encouraged to read the appraisals in the appendices in order to assess the validity and applicability of the research.

THE QUALITY OF THE RESEARCH EVIDENCE

Despite a number of randomised controlled trials having been published in this area, there are a number of inadequacies in the research.

- Many of the studies are affected by referral bias, as parents were self-referring their children. They clearly could be considered to be the most motivated families and may not represent the average family that is referred to a clinic.

- Many of the reviewed studies do not provide adequate data on socio-economic status or the racial/ethnic status of the participants. As these families constitute a growing proportion of mental health referrals, matching families to treatments based on culture-specific variables is extremely important.

- At present much of the research includes children with 'behavioural problems'; future studies should attempt to ensure that the children enrolled are diagnosed with ODD or CD to provide consistent classification, which is crucial for scientific rigour and for the interpretation of results.

- The wide range of outcome measures used both within and between studies makes it difficult to assess meaningful changes in response to treatment. Many of the studies found significant results only because a large number of measurements were used: they did not necessarily find a decrease in the problem behaviour of the child. This is very misleading for the reader. The development of a core set of uniform outcome measures represents one of the most important challenges for researchers in many areas of child mental health, including those researching parent-training programmes.

- Potential bias is further introduced as parent reports were frequently used to assess the outcomes of programmes. The development of additional 'blind' assessors would add to the evaluation of these programmes.

- The length of follow-up used in the papers was relatively short, with the average being six months to one year. From Barlow's (1999) systematic review it was reported that long-term follow-up to assess whether behaviours were maintained over time ranged from six months to three years. None of the studies, however, provided evidence concerning the relationship between the initial severity of the problems or the duration of the programme and effects over time.

ESTIMATING THE EFFECT OF INTERVENTIONS

Effect size

One difficulty with interpreting the effect of an intervention is that a number of different outcomes are often measured within the same study; it can also be difficult to combine the results of several studies that have used different ways of measuring similar concepts. These problems are commonly faced in evaluating the psychological literature. For instance, in estimating the effect of an intervention such as parent training for children with conduct disorder, we may be interested in examining the effects on the children's behaviour as rated by both their parents and teachers, on their self-esteem, on their peer relationships, on their likelihood of being excluded from school and so on. It is also likely that, if we are summarising a series of studies that have tested this intervention, they will have measured different aspects of these outcomes and will have used a variety of measures to do so. One way of summarising these data either across outcomes or across studies is to use what are called 'effect sizes'.

The mathematical relationships between a number of different estimates of effect, including correlation coefficients and various measures of statistical significance, mean that estimates of effect size can be produced from data of many different types, including both continuous and dichotomous data. These can then be combined either within or across studies to produce a single average effect size to describe the effect of a particular intervention. For this summary effect size to be meaningful requires an assumption that the intervention has some overall average effect which is similar across different outcomes, different measures and different studies, estimates of which vary between these only by chance.

Cohen (1981) argued that the meaning of effect size (d) could be directly interpreted: he suggested that it could be thought of as 'small' when $d = 0.2$, 'medium' when $d = 0.5$ and 'large' when $d = 0.8$. It has, however, been pointed out subsequently that this depends on what quantity is being estimated by the effect size.

As with any measure of the magnitude of an effect, it is possible to calculate a confidence interval around an effect size. This is obviously desirable but is often omitted by authors, although it can be estimated if samples sizes are provided.

This idea that effect size is a useful way of interpreting the magnitude of the effect of an intervention has led to its widespread use both for summarising data and for reporting the magnitude of single estimates in the social science and psychological literature. While many clinicians may have difficulty in interpreting the meaning of different effect sizes, the same is probably true of estimates of the absolute differences on many of the scales employed in studies in this area. In this report we have included the effect sizes and their confidence limits where these have been provided by the authors.

P values

P values indicate the probability that any particular outcome would have arisen by chance. A P value of less than 1 in 20 ($P < 0.05$) is considered (by convention – although it is in fact arbitrary) 'statistically significant' and a P value of less than 1 in 100 ($P < 0.01$) as 'highly significant'. However, one incorrect chance association in 20 will seem to be significant when it is not and one in a 100 will seem highly significant when it is really a 'fluke'. A *P* value in the non-significant range tells you either that there is no difference between the groups or that there were too few subjects to demonstrate that such a difference existed. It does not tell you which.

If a finding is shown to be statistically significant, it is simply an indication of the probability or likelihood that there was a difference – any difference of any size. Statistical significance indicates that the observed difference is not actually zero. It is incorrect to assume that just because a finding is statistically significant, it must therefore be important. Clinical significance (importance) and statistical significance are not the same thing.

USING THE RESEARCH EVIDENCE

The next three chapters in this report are based on the research evidence discussed in this chapter. Where a reference is printed as (author, date**), this indicates that the paper has been appraised and a full appraisal can be found in Appendix 3. Where a reference is printed as (author, date*), this indicates that the paper was appraised in one of the systematic reviews included in the report. Appraisals of the papers included in Jane Barlow's review can be found in Appendix 4.

the research base for
parent-training programmes

Key messages

- Behavioural parent-training programmes, both individual and group programmes, are the most effective in reducing conduct disorders in young children.
- Group parent-training programmes are more cost-effective than individual programmes and provide the parents with peer support.
- The most evaluated parent-training programmes to date, which appear to be effective, are the Webster-Stratton programmes.
- The long-term effectiveness of parent-training programmes is not conclusively established.
- There is a need for the development of a strategy for the implementation and assessment of empirically supported programmes in general clinical settings.

Recent systematic reviews of parent-training have established that these programmes change parenting practice and that this is beneficial in terms of children's behaviour (Barlow, 1997, 1999**; NHS Centre for Reviews and Dissemination, 1997; Brestan & Eyberg, 1998**).

One of the NHS priorities for research is controlled studies of the efficacy and cost-effectiveness of psychological treatments for emotional and behavioural problems in young people. Also, the relationship of parenting skills to children's behaviour, and the development of strategies to improve the parenting of young children, have been highlighted as part of the Department of Health's strategy to improve the health of mothers and children (NHS Central Research and Development Committee, 1995).

WHAT TYPES OF PARENT-TRAINING PROGRAMMES ARE AVAILABLE?

Barlow & Stewart-Brown (2000) provide a historical perspective on parent-training programmes. The clinical use of parents as modifiers of their children's behaviour began in the 1960s, when it was shown that parents could successfully produce a wide range of behavioural changes in their children using behaviour modification techniques. One of the main advantages of using parents to change their children's behaviour was that this method overcame difficulties relating to the

---

References cited as (author, year**) are appraised in Appendix 3. References cited as (author, year*) have been appraised in one of the systematic reviews included in the report.

transfer of behaviour changes produced in the clinic to the home. It was also cost-effective and it seemed to eliminate some of the stigma associated with clinic attendance (Johnson & Katz, 1973). The use of groups to train parents began in the 1970s and over the past 10 years there has been a huge increase in the number of group-based parent-training programmes available, with the growing involvement of voluntary organisations in the provision of such programmes (Pugh *et al*, 1994).

A number of terms are used interchangeably to describe the same types of parent programmes. These include: parent-education programmes, parent-training programmes, parenting programmes and parent skills training. This report uses the term parent-training programme to mean any of the above. Although there are many variations of parent-training programmes, a number share common characteristics (Kazdin, 1993): the training is conducted primarily with the parents, who directly implement procedures at home, and there is usually no direct intervention by the therapist or trainer with the child.

Smith (1996) distinguishes two types of parent-training programmes: behavioural and relationship. However, the categories are not exclusive and many contemporary programmes combine elements of both the behavioural and the relationship programmes.

Relationship programmes

Examples of relationship-type programmes for general behaviour problems include:

- Parent–Infant Network (PIPPIN);

- Parent Effectiveness Training (PET);

- Systematic Training for Effective Parenting (STEP);

- NEWPIN;

- Family Caring Trust;

- Family Nurturing Network.

Relationship programmes are based on one of the following types of theory: humanistic, Adlerian, psychodynamic and family systems.

Humanistic approach

An example of this is PET. PET focuses on the communication of feelings and the cooperative resolution of parent–child conflicts (Gordon, 1975). PET is built on the premise that individuals will act in accord with their inherent desire to do what is right, based on the humanistic theory of Carl Rogers (1951). This approach is designed to facilitate parental attitude change and to equip parents with the skills necessary to put these newly acquired attitudes into action. PET regards maladaptive communication patterns as the primary cause of inappropriate child behaviour and assumes that improved relationships between parents and child will result if parents acquire three techniques:

- *Active listening*. The parent learns to listen to the child's concerns in a non-judgemental and accepting manner, in order to help the child understand, accept and deal with feelings or concerns. Parents learn the steps to good communication, which include ordering, threatening, lecturing, criticising and praising.

- *I-messages*. These are statements of the parent's feelings, communicated without blame. Included within the statement are a non-judgemental description of the child's behaviour and a description of the tangible effect of the child's behaviour on the parent.

- *No-lose method of negotiation*. This respects the child's needs and abilities to problem solve. It involves six steps: defining the conflict, brainstorming, evaluating alternatives, finding an alternative that satisfies both parties, deciding how to implement it and evaluating the outcome (Gordon, 1975).

Adlerian approach

This approach is based on the assumption that all human behaviour occurs for a social purpose and that, from childhood, belonging to a social unit is an individual's primary goal in life (Adler, 1927, 1930). The aims of Adlerian parent-training programmes are:

- to help parents understand the importance of mutual respect and understanding;

- to increase parents' awareness of the need to live together democratically as social equals in the family unit;

- to help parents understand that behaviour is contextual, goal-directed and socially orientated;

- to encourage behaviours that develop self-reliant, responsible and cooperative relationships within the family;

- to teach parents to guide their children by establishing firm, clear and consistent limits for all the family members.

A variation of the Adlerian approach shows parents how to identify the child's goal and how to respond to the misbehaviour (Dreikurs & Soltz, 1964). This approach teaches parents that a misbehaving child is a discouraged child and instructs parents how to use encouragement rather than praise to change behaviour. Parents are also taught to use natural and logical consequences instead of rewards and punishments.

Another modification to this approach is the STEP programme (Dinkmeyer & McKay, 1976). This is a skills-training version that combines Adlerian concepts with the communication skills necessary for effective parenting.

Psychodynamic theory

Programmes based on a psychodynamic model emphasise the importance of understanding the influence of past relationships in terms of current relationships and behaviour.

Family systems theory

These programmes aim to help parents understand their own behaviour and that of other family members and to locate the problem behaviour of their children within the context of relationships at home and at school.

Behavioural programmes

These programmes place an emphasis on teaching parents skills that will enable them to change the events leading up to the problem behaviour and the consequences that are causing and maintaining the problem behaviour in the child (Skinner, 1953). With the development of social learning theory (Patterson, 1982), behavioural programmes began to be supplemented with other methods, which take into account parental cognition and place the child within a systemic context.

Individual programmes

Patterson's (1982) work at the Oregon Social Learning Center was extremely influential in developing parenting programmes. The Center saw over 2000 families over two decades and produced some of the first and most powerful research on conduct-disordered children. Their first programme was designed for parents of children aged 3–12 years and included the following elements:

- identifying and recording problematic child behaviours at home;

- using positive reinforcement techniques;

- applying discipline methods such as removal of privileges and 'time-out';

- supervising and monitoring child behaviour;

- negotiating and problem-solving strategies and the design of individual programmes.

These management skills are taught step by step, with each newly learnt skill forming the basis for the next. This programme involves approximately 20 hours of direct contact with individual families and includes home visits. Recently the programme has been developed to include adolescent problem behaviours; initial results seem positive (Patterson & Forgatch, 1995).

Forehand & McMahon (1981) modified an extremely influential programme by Hanf (1969, cited in McMahon, 1994), which addressed non-compliance in young children (3–8 years). They went on to evaluate the programme and found significant results after up to 14 years of follow-up (Long *et al*, 1994). The programme takes place in a playroom, which is equipped with a one-way mirror, and the parents are supported and instructed in their interactions via an earpiece. A therapist works individually with the parents and the child. Initially parents are taught how to play with their children in a non-directive (child-centred) way and how to identify and reward pro-social behaviour through praise and attention. Parents then learn ways of giving instructions geared to reduce the possibility of a defiant response and punishing non-compliance by time-out.

This parent–child interaction therapy has been examined further by Eyberg *et al* (1995*). Their programme used the same principles as Hanf (1969) and Forehand & McMahon (1981) but instead of limiting the programme to 8–10 sessions, their programme had no time limit. The programme terminated when: parents demonstrated mastery of skills; parents reported that the presenting problems were resolved; the child no longer met the criteria for ODD; or when parents reported they felt ready to terminate.

Examples of behavioural programmes for general behaviour problems include:

- ABC of Behaviour;

- Seven Supertactics for Parents;

- The Parents and Children Series;

- Promoting Positive Parenting.

Behavioural (group-based) programme with elements from relationship approaches

As a way of creating a cost-effective and more widely available programme, the Seattle Parenting Clinic research team decided on a group discussion videotape modelling programme (GDVM) as a parent-training programme for young conduct-disordered children (aged 3–8 years) (Webster-Stratton, 1984*).

The BASIC parent-training programme contains components of the Forehand & McMahon (1981) and Patterson (1982) programmes, as well as problem-solving and communication skills (the programme incorporates non-violent discipline components, such as time-out, logical and natural consequences and monitoring, plus the strategic use of differential attention, encouragement and praise). It consists of a series of 10 videotape programmes, modelling parenting skill areas. There are 250 vignettes, which give examples of positive and negative parent–child interactions, each of which lasts approximately one to two minutes. A therapist shows the vignettes to groups of 8–12 parents. After each vignette, the therapist leads the group discussion of the relevant interactions and encourages parents' ideas and problem solving as well as role play and rehearsal. Homework exercises are given to parents to practise a range of skills at home. Children do not attend the programme. Webster-Stratton & Herbert (1993, 1994) emphasise that parent groups address important risk factors for child conduct disorder, family isolation and stigmatisation, and provide peer support. Throughout the BASIC course, the group's mutual support is extended to include 'buddy calls', in which parents call each other to share experiences.

The programme has also been used by parents of conduct-disordered children as a self-administered intervention, viewing the video vignettes and completing the homework assignment without therapist feedback or group support. The programmes were targeted at high-risk families, including those enrolled on Head Start programmes (Webster-Stratton, 1998**), which are discussed further in Chapter 5.

WHICH TYPE OF PROGRAMME IS MORE EFFECTIVE IN TREATING CONDUCT DISORDER?

Behavioural interventions based on social learning principles are among the best and the most thoroughly evaluated interventions available to assist children with conduct disorders (Brestan & Eyberg, 1998**; Taylor & Biglan, 1998; Sanders et al, 2000**). A variety of different formats (as mentioned previously) have been shown to be effective (Forehand & McMahon, 1981; Webster-Stratton, 1990b).

The two reviews appraised and commented on in this report are Brestan & Eyberg (1998**) and Barlow (1999**). Brestan & Eyberg (1998**) reviewed the literature on all psychosocial interventions (individual and group) for all child and adolescent conduct disorders, including ODD and CD, for the whole age range. The Barlow (1999**) systematic review, on the other hand, focused on group-based parent-training programmes only, for children between the ages of 3 and 10 years with behavioural problems, including studies where children were diagnosed with ODD and CD.

In the Brestan & Eyberg (1998**) review, all treatments were judged according to the criteria for well established and probably efficacious treatments as originally defined by the Task Force on Promotion and Dissemination of Psychological Procedures (1995) (see also Chambless et al, 1996).

Two treatment approaches were found to have strong empirical support for children with conduct disorders and were classified as 'treatments identified as well established'. The first is a parent-training programme based on Patterson & Guillion's (1968*) manual, *Living with Children*. This treatment was judged to have a robust effect demonstrated in studies by different research teams. The programme is based on operant principles of behaviour change and is designed to teach parents to monitor targeted deviant behaviours, monitor and reward incompatible behaviours, and ignore or punish deviant behaviours of their child. Treatments using the lessons from *Living with Children* have generally been short-term behavioural parent-training programmes and have been compared with other treatments for children with conduct disorder (e.g. psychodynamic) in addition to no-treatment control groups. The study participants have included both boys and girls from a broad age range, including those who had been referred from juvenile courts.

The second treatment identified as 'well established' was more specific to younger children: Webster-Stratton's parent-training programme of videotape modelling. This programme is administered to parents with therapist-led group discussion. The treatment has been tested in several studies, in which it has been compared with waiting-list control groups and alternative parent-training formats (Spaccarelli et al, 1992*; Webster-Stratton, 1984*, 1994**; Webster-Stratton et al, 1988*). The studies typically included both boys and girls in the 4–8-year age range who had been selected for treatment based on either parent referral for behavioural problems or diagnostic criteria for ODD or CD.

A number of treatments in the Brestan & Eyberg (1998**) review were found to have the necessary empirical support to be judged 'probably efficacious'. These included parent–child treatments based on Hanf's (1969) two-stage behavioural treatment model for pre-school children (Wells & Egan, 1988*; McNeil et al, 1991*; Eyberg et al, 1995*). Another programme in this category was the delinquency prevention programme (Tremblay et al, 1995*). This programme is also designed for pre-school children; however, it does not focus on parent-training and so is not appraised in this report.

Barlow's (1997, 1999**) systematic review reviewed three meta-analyses (Cedar & Levant, 1990*; Serketich & Dumas, 1996*; Todres & Bunston, 1993*) and 16 randomised controlled trials (including two follow-up studies). Barlow critically appraised the design of each of the three meta-analyses and the 16 randomised controlled studies (not the two follow-up studies). Summary tables of the critical appraisals for each of these can be found in Appendix 4. As the author discusses, and as can be seen from the tables, there were a number of methodological problems in the majority of studies. The review discusses the results of the studies logically, and concludes that, while all group-based programmes produced changes in children's behaviour, the more 'behavioural' type of programme appeared to produce the best results (Karoly & Rosenthal, 1977*; Bernal *et al*, 1980*; Firestone *et al*, 1980*; Pinsker & Geoffroy, 1981*; Webster-Stratton, 1984*; Daly *et al*, 1985*; Scott & Stradling, 1987*; Webster-Stratton *et al*, 1988*; Lawes, 1992*; Spaccarelli *et al*, 1992*; Sutton, 1992*; Mullen *et al*, 1994*; Cunningham *et al*, 1995*). The review found overall that behavioural parent-training programmes are sufficiently well researched and their effectiveness well demonstrated. Barlow (1999**) does, however, suggest that the 'relationship' programmes may be more effective than the behavioural types in producing changes in parental attitudes, self-esteem and psychopathology and that, therefore, there is a need to examine their comparative effectiveness.

ARE GROUP PROGRAMMES BETTER THAN INDIVIDUAL PROGRAMMES?

As Barlow (1999**) discusses in her review, the Webster-Stratton studies 'provide a coherent and methodologically rigorous examination, of one particular type of parent-training programme'. Videotape modelling in both an individual and group setting was effective in terms of parent report and independent observations of children's behaviour. In Webster-Stratton's (1984*) study, the individual modelling programme was more cost-effective, because it was self-administered. However, in later studies Webster-Stratton *et al* (1988*) compared an individually administered videotape modelling method with a group discussion, and with a group discussion and videotape modelling method. While there were very few significant differences between the treatment groups in the short term, the findings consistently favoured group discussion with videotape modelling, while the individual videotape modelling was more cost-effective. Follow-up showed that at one year the group discussion with videotape modelling programme produced the best results and that after three years the group discussion with videotape modelling (GDVM) group was the only one showing 'stable improvements'. Two later studies (Webster-Stratton & Hammond, 1997**; Webster-Stratton, 1998**) confirm these findings and are discussed in more detail later in the report.

As well as Webster-Stratton's studies, Barlow's (1999**) review includes four other studies in which group-based programme were compared with individual therapy (Evans, 1976*; Lawes, 1992*; Sutton, 1992*; Cunningham *et al*, 1995*). Cunningham *et al* (1995*) and Lawes (1992*) both found that while individual parent-training was effective compared with a control group, no individual programme achieved the level of change produced by the group-based programmes. Sutton (1992*) showed that, irrespective of the method of administration and whether group or individual, a behavioural programme produced significant changes in children's behaviour.

Evans (1976*) compared a clinic-based programme working with individual parents with a community-based group programme and a waiting-list control group. Parents reported significant differences in favour of the community-based group, though observations of children's behaviour produced similar changes for both treatment groups and the control group. The advantage of the community-based group was that it was six times more cost-effective than the clinic programme, and it is suggested that families may have used this group who would not have used the individual clinic-based programme. As Barlow (1999**) points out, the method used in the study is a confounding variable, as it is not clear whether the method (group/individual) or the setting (community/group) is the decisive factor in producing change.

Besides cost, which obviously favours group training, group parent-training has a number of other benefits. Smith (1996) lists a number of these:

- groups help socially isolated families meet others;

- groups build a sense of cohesiveness;

- groups provide opportunities to share views and learn from others;

- groups provide appropriate role models;

- groups provide support;

- groups can be powerful in developing confidence and self-esteem.

LONG-TERM OUTCOMES OF THESE PROGRAMMES

Barlow (1997, 1999**) found that follow-up reports of maintenance of the change in behaviour ranged from six months (Scott & Stradling, 1987*; Spaccarelli et al, 1992*; Cunningham et al, 1995*), to one year (Webster-Stratton, 1984*; Webster-Stratton et al, 1989*), two years (Bernal et al, 1980*) and three years (Daly et al, 1985*; Webster-Stratton, 1990c*). Longer follow-ups are rarely used, although one programme reported maintenance of gains 10–14 years later (Long et al, 1994).

It should be noted that these studies used only parent report measures to assess long-term effectiveness. Also, despite showing that the effects of parenting programmes were enduring over time in terms of children's behaviour, in at least one study up to a third of parents continued to experience problems with their children's behaviour (Webster-Stratton, 1990c*). However, this study showed that families who continued to have problems were characterised by single-parent status, increased maternal depression, lower social class and a family history of alcoholism and drug misuse. Barlow (1999**) noted that none of the included studies provided evidence concerning the relationship between the initial severity of the problems or the duration of the programme and the maintenance of effects over time.

ARE PROGRAMMES EFFECTIVE IN GENERAL CLINICAL SETTINGS?

Most of the research has been conducted under ideal research conditions. It is important to know whether interventions that are effective in a research or clinical setting can also be effective within other settings, such as family, education and juvenile justice settings. It is difficult to generalise from one group to another.

Weisz et al (1995) criticise Webster-Stratton's BASIC Parents and Children's Series (PACS) programme on the grounds that the evaluations were offered in a university setting (rather than in a clinic) with, it could be argued, a homogeneous population (families with children having conduct disorders) receiving help from a university research clinic. These factors could account for the success of the programme. Therefore, could similar results be obtained in a general clinical setting?

Taylor *et al* (1998**) argue that there is little evidence that services usually offered in typical applied settings are effective. They report on Weisz *et al*'s (1995) review of child therapy outcomes. Two hundred controlled studies were identified that had shown that university-based treatment works, yet only nine clinic-based controlled studies were identified and the average effect size of these studies was zero. Only two of the nine published studies were completed in the past 25 years and only one of these two was a randomised controlled trial. The authors concluded that they did not know whether traditional child therapy was effective.

Taylor *et al* (1998**) evaluated the effectiveness of the PACS programme in an independent setting, hypothesising that it would be more effective than no treatment in reducing child behaviour problems and more effective than the typical eclectic treatment used in the clinic to improve children's behaviour problems. The PACS programme, as with other Webster-Stratton programmes, has features that have potential for success in applied settings. These features include special pre-therapy training of therapists and a highly structured pre-planned training manual. Results indicated that the PACS programme could be successfully implemented in an applied setting and that it was more effective than either no treatment or the eclectic treatment in reducing reports of child behaviour problems. It should be noted that there were methodological problems with the study design. Despite these limitations, the authors note that the study offers one of the first direct comparisons of typical service in a children's mental health setting with an empirically validated intervention developed in a research setting. The authors discuss the need to identify a strategy for implementing empirically supported therapy in applied settings and suggest that further research is needed to identify critical components of successful evidence-based therapy to guide its implementation in applied settings. Professionals are currently exploring how to transfer these approaches successfully from a clinic setting into the community either by working with individual families (Davis & Spurr, 1998) or by employing a group format.

the research base for improving the effectiveness of parent-training programmes

> *Key messages*
>
> - Addressing parental problems alongside parent-training programmes has produced inconclusive results regarding its effectiveness in improving a child's behaviour.
> - Child social skills training in addition to the parent-training programme may well maintain a decrease in conduct disorders over time better than parent-training programmes alone.
> - Approximately 40% of parents drop out of parent-training programmes. Making services more accessible by running them in a non-clinical setting or where services have good transport links may improve attendance rates. Providing appropriate services for ethnic minority families and supporting isolated mothers in the community are other factors to be considered in an attempt to improve attendance at parent-training programmes.
> - The delivery of parent-training programmes needs to be considered carefully to increase parent participation.

ARE THERE ADDITIONAL INTERVENTIONS TO INCREASE THE EFFECTIVENESS OF PROGRAMMES?

There is growing need within intervention programmes such as parent management training to include other interventions that address parental distress, depression and family functioning. Many young children with conduct disorders have parents with significant personal problems (Webster-Stratton, 1989, 1994**; Sanders *et al*, 2000**). In these cases behavioural interventions alone are unlikely to help. Other interventions, such as child social skills training and programmes involving teachers and schools, have also been shown to increase the effectiveness of parent-training programmes (Webster-Stratton, 1993, 1998**; Webster-Stratton & Hammond, 1997**).

The Positive Parenting of Preschoolers (Triple P) programme has been developed in Australia and has been shown to be effective with young children (three-year-olds) who have behaviour problems (Sanders & Markie-Dadds, 1996; Sanders *et al*, 2000**). The programme aims to promote positive caring relationships between children and their parents by: improving parenting skills; increasing

> References cited as (author, year**) are appraised in Appendix 3. References cited as (author, year*) have been appraised in one of the systematic reviews included in the report.

parents' sense of competence; improving communication between parents regarding parenting; and reducing parental stress.

The programme incorporates five levels of intervention. The different levels enable the intervention to be tailored to the assessed needs and preferences of individual families (Marshall & Watt, 1999).

- Level 1 includes information-based strategies using the medium that targets the whole population about parenting and promoting a child's development.

- Level 2 (selective Triple P) is a one- or two-session brief consultation programme for use in anticipatory well-child care for parents with specific concerns about their child's behaviour or development.

- Level 3 (primary care Triple P) is a four-session brief consultation model for use in a primary care setting such as child health services and family medicine for parents with specific concerns and who require consultations or active skills training.

- Level 4 (standard Triple P, group Triple P or self-help Triple P) is an intensive parenting skills programme that can be delivered in any of the three models and is for parents wanting intensive training in positive parenting skills. This level typically targets severe behaviour problems.

- Level 5 (enhanced Triple P) provides additional interventions for families with concurrent child behaviour problems and adult adjustment problems, such as depression, stress or conflict between parents (Sanders *et al*, 2000**).

The Sanders *et al* (2000**) study was designed to examine the effects of targeting marital conflict and parental depression in family-based early-intervention programmes for children at high risk of developing conduct disorders. The enhanced Triple P (level 5) and standard Triple P (level 4) were associated with lower levels of parent-reported disruptive child behaviour, lower levels of dysfunctional parenting and greater parental competence compared with a waiting-list group. The mothers in the enhanced Triple P condition reported fewer child behaviour problems compared with all the other conditions on the Parent Daily Report measure. At one-year follow-up, groups on the enhanced and standard programmes showed greater improvement on parent-observed disruptive child behaviour. The authors conclude that although the study was designed as an early-intervention trial rather than as a prevention trial, its findings inform their goal, which is the implementation and evaluation of their model as a universal, accessible, high-quality, low-cost, multidisciplinary prevention strategy to enhance competent parenting.

Research by Webster-Stratton *et al* (1989) and Webster-Stratton & Hammond (1990, 1999) also found that parental, personal and interpersonal factors play a role in the formation of conduct disorders, and therefore need a broader parenting programme. Family factors such as life stress, socio-economic status and relationship conflict were found to determine whether children's behaviour improved (Webster-Stratton & Hammond, 1990). Two more recent programmes, which are not included in Barlow's (1999**) review, were developed to supplement the BASIC programme: ADVANCE (Webster-Stratton, 1994**), which examined the parents' relationship, and PARTNERS I (Webster-Stratton, 1998**), which looked at strategies for supporting children's academic learning, including involving teachers in the programme (the latter is discussed in more detail in Chapter 5).

The ADVANCE programme consists of a further six videotapes, which focus on family issues other than parenting skills. These include: anger management, coping with depression, marital communication skills, problem-solving strategies, and how to teach children to problem solve and manage their anger more effectively. As with the BASIC programme, children do not attend sessions and homework is given to the parents to carry out with their children (Webster-Stratton, 1984*). Webster-Stratton's (1994**) study showed that although further work addressing parental problems produced significant improvements in parents' problem-solving, communication and collaboration skills, it failed to produce improved outcomes on measures of child behaviour.

Despite the findings of significant improvement in the child's behaviour at home lasting up to three years after their parents' attendance at the BASIC and in some cases ADVANCE courses, teachers found this improvement did not generalise to the classroom (Webster-Stratton & Hammond, 1997**). This led to the examination of the role that child factors played in the development and maintenance of conduct disorders. The 'Dinosaur Curriculum' was designed as a social skills training programme for children aged 3–8 years (Webster-Stratton, 1996). It was found that, combined with BASIC, its impact on children's behaviour after one year was superior to that of BASIC or child training alone (Webster-Stratton & Hammond, 1997**). The Dinosaur Curriculum consists of hand puppets for role play and over 100 vignettes on videotape. The sessions are aimed at improving children's behaviour at home and at school, social competence, and peer interactions, including non-aggressive conflict management strategies and how to develop friendships.

Work showing particular promise is that in which parent education is carried out alongside interventions with the child in school (Mental Health Foundation, 1999). Programmes involving teachers in training as well as parents, to ensure consistency in discipline and management between the home and school environments, seem effective (Webster-Stratton, 1998**). Parent-training programmes involving schools is discussed in more detail in Chapter 5.

Non-responders also need to be examined. Little attention has been given to this group, even in terms of their characteristics.

WHAT FACTORS INFLUENCE PARENTS' PARTICIPATION IN PARENT-TRAINING PROGRAMMES?

Patterson & Chamberlain (1988) propose that for any of these parent-training programmes to be effective, the active participation of parents in parent skills training is necessary. Research suggests that despite parent-training programmes having a positive effect in improving behaviour problems in children, there does appear to be a major problem of adherence to treatment. Many families who begin treatment in mental health services leave before the treatment is completed (Forehand et al, 1983; Webster-Stratton & Hammond, 1990; Offord et al, 1998). Kazdin (1996) found that 40–60% of families who begin treatment leave before completion. A reason for this, as Lloyd (1999) points out, is that many of the studies are based on samples containing high-risk families, such as single parents in receipt of social security benefit, mothers reporting depression, spouse or child abuse, alcoholism or drug misuse, and parents with prior involvement with the child protection services (Scott & Stradling, 1987; Webster-Stratton et al, 1988; Webster-Stratton, 1989, 1990b). These factors (which have been discussed in Chapter 1) are associated with an increased risk of conduct disorders.

There is a need to make services more accessible; many parents are uncomfortable or unwilling to label their child with a mental health problem. Before group-based work was as prolific as it is today, Farrington (1977) noted that in some cases labelling a child and the stigmatisation of attending a clinical setting led to the escalation of antisocial behaviour. Cunningham *et al* (1995*) found that parents are more likely to participate in group-based parenting services than family-based services in clinical settings. Therefore families should be assigned to group parent-training (in which there is a good likelihood of responding) rather than individual training (unless there are a larger number of risk factors). It may be that families need to be divided into those who are offered group parent-training programmes and those who may need more individual parent treatments before the group parent-training programmes.

Prinz & Miller (1996) see parent participation as comprising not only rate (frequency of attendance and dropout) but also quality (parent engagement with the group and group leader during training sessions). Orrell-Valente *et al* (1999) suggest other important influences on parent participation. These include: the nature of the relationship between therapist and parent; parent and family characteristics; and the extent to which the parent likes the programme and finds its content relevant.

There has been considerable research into the factors causing some parents to drop out of programmes. Kazdin (1990) showed that termination from treatment was linked with: more severe conduct disorder symptoms; mothers reporting greater stress from their relationship with the child and life events; and families being at greater socio-economic disadvantage. Situational constraints may also arise, for example unreliable transportation, competing obligations or other siblings needing to be looked after (Orrell-Valente *et al*, 1999).

Child factors

Pre-school children appear to have the highest rates of positive response to parent-training programmes (Barclay, 1997). The severity of the child's behavioural problem has in some studies been correlated with more limited treatment efficacy and a greater likelihood of parental premature termination from training (Dumas, 1984; Holden *et al*, 1990). This has, however, been explained in another way: the severity of the child's problem is simply serving as a marker for more important parent factors that are actually the reason for parents terminating training prematurely or failing to respond positively to the training (Barclay, 1997).

Parent factors

Parents who are younger than average, left school at a young age and are lower in social class do not usually achieve the same degree of success as others (Webster-Stratton & Hammond, 1990). Orrell-Valente *et al* (1999) suggest that parents of lower socio-economic status must contend with more income-related stressors, making participation in an intervention unlikely. However, Webster-Stratton (1998**) found that only 17% of the 'low-income' families in her study did not attend at least 50% of the sessions. Holden *et al* (1990) found that the family's ethnic group was associated with dropping out of treatment or progressing more slowly through training.

Single-parent families respond less well to parent-training programmes than two-parent households. Single parents face additional stressors and lack support from intimate partners (Barclay, 1997). Diminished benefits from parent-training and high drop-out rates are especially likely for mothers who are socially isolated from adult peers in their community and encounter aversive interactions with their extended family.

It has been shown that maternal isolation, when combined with socio-economic disadvantage, accounts for nearly 50% of the variance in treatment effectiveness (Dumas & Wahler, 1983). By providing greater involvement and training from the therapist, ensuring more time for practice and addressing the mothers' social isolation either before or during training, these families may be able achieve significant improvements in child management (Dumas & Wahler, 1983; Dadds & McHugh, 1992).

Parents with serious forms of psychopathology seem not to do well in parent-training programmes. They often start out with resistance to the training and homework assignments and seem to remain so throughout treatment (Barclay, 1997). Parents who show signs of depression and helplessness or poor anger control typically do not respond as positively in such training programmes and are more likely to drop out of treatment. It has been suggested that providing training in more effective problem-solving or anger management skills before or as an adjunct to parent-training in child management may prove useful in enhancing the effectiveness of parent-training programmes.

The degree of marital discord is also a predictor of decreased effectiveness of the parent-training programme. In cases where marital discord is apparent, it may be better to provide parents with marital therapy or divorce counselling to help resolve their marital problems either before parent-training in child management is offered or as an adjunct to it. As previously mentioned, Webster-Stratton's (1994**) study showed that although the ADVANCE programme produced significant improvements in parent's problem solving, communication and collaboration skills, it failed to produce improved outcomes on measures of child behaviour.

Therapist factors

Parent trainers working with families of seriously antisocial children can expect to encounter resistance. Resistance can occur in response both to the formal training procedures within the session and to the homework assignments parents are required to perform (Barclay, 1997). According to Patterson & Chamberlain (1988, 1994), 'family coordinators' are at risk of interpreting parents' resistance as personal rejection. However, if they recognise that parents' resistance is a normative part of the change process and retain their objectivity towards parents, they will be more likely to continue to serve parents effectively.

Research in individual therapy shows that the quality of the therapist–client working alliance predicts client participation (Bordin, 1979; Horvath, 1994). Orrell-Valente et al (1999) hypothesised that the quality of the therapeutic relationship that develops between the therapist and parent may well be a primary influence on the parent's attendance at group sessions, as well as on the parent's level of interest and involvement with the group and therapist during these training sessions.

In Orrell-Valente et al's (1999) study the degree to which therapists remained engaged in the therapeutic relationship had important associations with the rate and quality of parent participation in this type of intervention. It is important that the therapist is liked, respected and trusted by the parents. It has also emerged from research that the demographic similarity between the therapist and the parent and the therapist's life experiences are relevant to the parent group (Orrell-Valente et al, 1999). One of the conclusions drawn by these authors was that it is important to learn from parents the extent to which they like the programme and find its contents relevant to their needs.

The significance of these potential influences on parent participation is likely to be heightened for prevention programmes in which children are selected via school-based screening, in which services are delivered in a school/ community setting and in which parents are not initiating the request for help themselves (as will be described in Chapter 5). Therefore preventive programmes must include services that will minimise the impact of situational constraints and maximise parent participation (Orrell-Valente *et al*, 1999). In many preventive studies, programmes offer services such as transportation, child care and payment for attendance and/or completion of questionnaires (Conduct Problems Prevention Research Group, 1999*a***; Reid *et al*, 1999**).

five the research base for the prevention of conduct disorders

---

Key messages

- The research reviewed in this chapter suggests that the pre-school age may be a critical time, developmentally, at which to prevent the onset of conduct disorders.
- Negative school experiences can be a risk factor for conduct disorders; therefore many preventive programmes have been conducted in schools.
- Initial results from the LIFT and Fast Track programmes are inconclusive with regard to the effectiveness of preventive programmes. Webster-Stratton's PARTNERS (parent-training with teacher training) programme did, however, result in a decrease in conduct disorders for children in the intervention condition.

Previous chapters have shown that parent-training programmes appear to be effective in the management of conduct disorders in young children and in the prevention of conduct disorders. It seems that the efficacy of programmes can be improved by adding other dimensions, such as involving schools in order to increase the generalisability of the intervention with regard to the child's behaviour. Involving teachers and parents in children's behaviour management provides consistency in the child's discipline between the home and school. This chapter discusses the importance of prevention in pre-school children, in which parent-training programmes play an important role.

As has been discussed in Chapter 1, conduct disorders are multifactorially determined. Therefore preventive programmes must be comprehensive and target multiple risk and protective factors (Coie *et al*, 1993; Yoshikawa, 1994). Marshall & Watt (1999) emphasise the importance of focusing interventions on the mechanisms by which risk and protective factors operate, as change in these mechanisms will alter the development of problem behaviour. The ideal target for intervention is a risk factor present at one developmental period that has the greatest causal relationship for a risk factor at the next developmental period. As the authors discuss, research has not yet identified these periods. However, the period from infancy to pre-school appears to be one of the most critical in a child's development. Between the ages of five and seven years, children undergo a major developmental transformation, which generally includes increases in cognitive skills, as well as changes in brain size and function (White, 1965). This transition and the accompanying

---

References cited as (author, year**) are appraised in Appendix 3. References cited as (author, year*) have been appraised in one of the systematic reviews included in the report.

developmental changes allow children to undertake more responsibilities, independence and social roles (Belsky & MacKinnon, 1994). Therefore the relationships between affective understanding, cognition and behaviour are of crucial importance in socially competent action and healthy peer relations. Research seems to suggest that treating children at a pre-school age to prevent the onset of conduct disorders is the way forward; a number of studies have taken young children from high-risk groups and offered parent-training programmes to their families (Webster-Stratton, 1997, 1998**; Conduct Problems Prevention Research Group, 1999a**).

HIGH-RISK CHILDREN

Interventions aimed at reducing or preventing the precursors of juvenile delinquency, such as antisocial, aggressive, acting-out and moody behaviours in children, have shown some promising results (Zigler *et al*, 1992). Many of the early childhood intervention programmes were originally designed to address goals other than delinquency, although several studies included outcomes on delinquency or related factors: Yale Child Welfare Research Program (Provence & Naylor, 1983); Houston Parent–Child Development Center Program (Johnson, 1990); High/Scope Perry Preschool Program (Schweinhart & Weikart, 1997); Seattle Social Development Project (Hawkins *et al*, 1992); and Montreal Longitudinal-Experimental Study (Tremblay *et al*, 1992). More recent studies have specifically addressed the prevention of conduct disorders (Webster-Stratton, 1998**; Conduct Problems Prevention Research Group, 1999a**; Reid *et al*, 1999**).

Head Start is a comprehensive programme for pre-school children and families living in poverty. It has four key components: education, social services, parent involvement, and health (Zigler *et al*, 1994). Children in the Head Start population are at higher than average risk of developing conduct disorders because the risk factors are present at higher than average rates (McLoyd, 1990). Research with Head Start has examined the impact of programmes on children's cognitive development and academic readiness, although few studies have examined Head Start's potential effects on enhancing children's social competence or reducing conduct disorders (Webster-Stratton, 1998**). Webster-Stratton also points out that although Head Start's work involves parents in the day-to-day operations, there had been no research examining the promotion of parenting skills or the provision of a mutual support network.

Webster-Stratton's (1998**) study examined the effectiveness of supplementing an established, theory-based parent-training programme with teacher training (PARTNERS) and using the combination as a selective intervention to prevent the development of ODD and CD in the Head Start population. The positive results for the intervention group indicated the benefits of using a clinic-based treatment programme (designed originally for parents with children with ODD/CD) as a prevention programme for a diverse and disadvantaged population who were not necessarily concerned with significant child behaviour problems. It was previously thought that 'low-income' parents were unlikely to attend parent groups, likely to drop out of programmes and likely to fail to show improvements in their parenting, but Webster Stratton's (1998**) findings provide new evidence in this regard. Only 17% of parents did not attend at least 50% of the sessions. Webster-Stratton (1998**) found that programmes that are community based (offered through the schools so that they are more accessible to parents living on welfare) and that are delivered collaboratively with teachers and family social workers result in a relatively high level of parental engagement. Parent-training programmes can result in parents gaining the knowledge, control and competence they need to cope effectively with the stresses of parenting under conditions of poverty. Webster-

Stratton (1998**) concludes that comprehensive parenting programmes spanning the pre-school to early school years and given at critical transition phases in later years would offer great potential for reducing conduct disorders and preventing delinquency in later years.

In addition to child factors and parenting practices, negative school experiences, particularly problematic peer relations and academic difficulties heighten the risk of a child developing antisocial behaviour (Conduct Problems Prevention Research Group, 1999a**). In the early school years, aggressive rejected children often show hostile attributional biases (Dodge *et al*, 1994), poor emotion regulation, unskilled social problem solving and a tendency to overestimate the positive consequences of aggression (Perry *et al*, 1986; Underwood, 1997). Peer rejection and academic difficulties at school entry can in turn increase conduct disorders (Coie & Dodge, 1998). Children whose skill deficits (both academic and social) persist across the early school years will face academic failure as well as increasingly provocative peer situations and gravitate towards friends who influence them into worsening antisocial behaviour, especially if they are living in high-crime neighbourhoods. Therefore interventions with high-risk children may need to continue across the transition from childhood to adolescence, and to provide more intensive intervention around the period when peer influence becomes strongest (Conduct Problems Prevention Research Group, 1999a**).

The LIFT school programme (Reid *et al*, 1999**) was designed to decrease the likelihood of aggressive children being rejected by the normative peer group, by improving peer interactions in the school context (such rejection increases the risk of subsequent conduct disorders and delinquency). The LIFT programme comprised 20 one-hour sessions over a 10-week period. Each session comprised four parts: classroom instruction and discussion on specific social and problem-solving skills; skills practice in small and large groups; unstructured play in the context of a group cooperation game; and review and the presentation of daily rewards. Parts 1, 2 and 4 of each session took place in the classroom and were structured by the LIFT teacher. To encourage the use of positive social and problem-solving skills and to discourage destructive behaviours during this time, a modification of the Good Behaviour Game (GBG) was used (Dolan *et al*, 1993). The GBG utilises groups that are created at the beginning of the programme; each class is divided into four or five groups, who are asked to sit together for small-group activities. During the GBG, group members work individually to earn rewards for their group and for their class. When a child is observed displaying a positive behaviour, a teacher or staff member identifies the behaviour and gives the child an armband. When a child is observed displaying a negative behaviour, that is logged on a chart. At the end of playtime, children place their armbands in a classroom jar. When the jar is full, the entire class earns a reward. The negative behaviours on the chart are tallied. This value is subtracted from a set of points that the group was given at the beginning of playtime. If the group manages to retain a preset amount of tokens, each member earns a sticker. Over time, when the group earns a set number of points, each individual in the group is allowed to select a prize from the class prize box.

To increase parental involvement in the experiences of their child at school, a telephone and answering machine were installed in each participating classroom and weekly newsletters were sent home about school LIFT activities. On the answering machines, teachers were asked to leave a brief daily message about class activities, special events and homework assignments. Parents could call at any time to hear the message or to leave a message for the teacher. Teachers could respond if appropriate.

The study did not produce any significant results between intervention and control groups with regard to a decrease in problem behaviours, although following intervention playground observations revealed a decrease in antisocial behaviour by the children in the experimental schools compared with the control schools.

Fast Track (Conduct Problems Prevention Research Group, 1999*a***) stands for 'Families And Schools Together'. It is a comprehensive, multi-site intervention designed to prevent serious and chronic antisocial behaviour in a sample of children selected at school entry as being at high risk because of their conduct disorders at kindergarten and home. The intervention is guided by a developmental theory positing the interaction of multiple influences on the development of antisocial behaviour. As well as these children having a number of environmental stresses and parenting problems, they often enter school poorly prepared for the social, emotional and cognitive demands of the setting. The children's parents are often unprepared to relate effectively with school staff and a poor home–school relationship often exacerbates the problem.

Fast Track was designed to identify high-risk children before their first year at school and to address the major deficits that lead to subsequent school failure, rejection by peers and increased aggression towards them, and disruptive and defiant behaviour towards authorities. Kindergarten provides the first occasion for the universal screening of children who are disruptive at home and at school. There are six components to the intervention for grade 1 children. The first five programmes are administered to the high-risk intervention subjects:

- parent-training groups designed to promote the development of positive family–school relationships and to teach parents behaviour management skills;

- home visits for the purpose of fostering parents' problem-solving skills, self-efficacy and life management;

- child social training groups;

- child tutoring in reading;

- child friendship enhancement in the classroom.

The sixth component is a teacher-led course (called PATHS), which is a universal intervention directed towards the development of emotional concepts, social understanding and self-control. The evaluation of this component is discussed separately, later (Conduct Problems Prevention Research Group, 1999*b***).

The results at the end of the first year indicate that better social skills and more positive peer relations were achieved as a result of the intervention. Intervention children developed better basic reading skills and better social and emotional coping skills than those in the control children. Intervention parents also demonstrated more positive involvement in their children's schools and more effective discipline strategies. There were, however, only partial, non-significant differences in the reduction of conduct disorders.

The LIFT programme and the Fast Track project were both costly; to increase the parent participation, parents were paid either to attend the sessions or to complete questionnaires. Although parent participation in both was high, there were no real significant decreases in problem behaviours in the intervention groups.

Looking specifically at the PATHS component, trials (using different versions of the PATHS curriculum) with both deaf and special-needs children have shown that the use of the PATHS curriculum is associated with significantly more mature social cognitions. Other findings have included better understanding of social problems, higher percentages of effective solutions, lower percentages of aggressive and passive solutions, and increased recognition of emotions (Greenberg & Kusche, 1993, 1998).

The Fast Track PATHS curriculum in grade 1 contained 57 lessons, approximately 80% of which were drawn from the published version of the curriculum (Kushe & Greenberg, 1994). Approximately 40% of the lessons in the Fast Track version of PATHS focus on skills related to understanding and communicating emotions (Conduct Problems Prevention Research Group, 1999b**). PATHS aims to teach young children to recognise the internal and external cues of affect and to label them with appropriate terms – 'feeling' words are identified. Other lessons help children understand the difference between feeling and behaviours. Children are given small cards with faces on and are asked to personalise their own 'feeling face' to allow them to communicate their feelings with minimal difficulty. Thirty per cent of the lessons focus on skills to increase positive social behaviour, such as making and sustaining friendships, using good manners, taking turns and sharing games. About a third of the programme focuses on self-control, affective awareness and communication, as well as problem-solving skills. In this section the Controls Signal Poster (CSP) is introduced. Children are taught that when they find themselves in a difficult, upsetting or frustrating situation they should stop/calm down, go slow/think, go/try my plan – as illustrated by the three colours of traffic lights. Lessons are typically conducted through a number of means, including discussions, role play, modelling stories and video presentations. Teachers are encouraged to generalise their use of PATHS concepts across the school day and to school settings outside the classroom.

In the study by the Conduct Problems Prevention Research Group (1999b**), which included all children in grade 1 classrooms from approximately 48 schools (not just the high-risk children as in the previously mentioned Fast Track study; Conduct Problems Prevention Research Group,1999a**), the results were more encouraging. The results themselves were described as conservative, as they did not include the high-risk sample in these analyses. Observer ratings found intervention classrooms to have a more positive atmosphere than control classrooms. Children in the intervention classrooms were found to have significantly better abilities in following rules and expressing feelings appropriately. The classroom's ability to stay focused on a task and the class's level of interest and enthusiasm were also significantly better in the intervention classrooms. The authors of the study note that the results may just be due to the fact that the teachers in the intervention classrooms were better teachers than those in the control classrooms. The intervention is currently being implemented through to grade 5, and so future results should minimise this potential bias.

The PATHS curriculum is currently being evaluated in the United Kingdom – see Chapter 6 for more information.

Universal programmes such as Head Start, Fast Track and the LIFT programme have the advantage of not labelling or stigmatising the children. The focus can be community-wide contextual factors and therefore it is easier to obtain support from the general public. Another advantage is that, as middle-class families also receive the intervention, the programmes have a better chance of running well, because middle-class families are more likely to complain about deficiencies in the programme and their complaints are more likely to be acted upon (Marshall & Watt, 1999). The disadvantages of universal interventions are that individuals are likely to obtain small benefits and that these programmes may be unnecessarily expensive, as a large number of children will receive the programme who may not actually need it.

Targeted interventions have major advantages in that they are potentially efficient if the targeting can be done accurately. However, targeted interventions also have disadvantages: how do you identify the children to target cost-effectively and accurately, and how can you screen for future behaviour? Another disadvantage of focusing on individuals most at risk may be the exclusion of effective community-level interventions (Offord *et al*, 1998). Results have also been shown to be better when both aggressive and non-aggressive children participate in the same groups (Dishion & Andrews, 1995).

evaluations of programmes and current research in the UK

Although there is a general consensus that parenting programmes seem to be effective, Pugh *et al* (1994) and Smith (1996) comment on the lack of rigorous studies evaluating the effectiveness of parent-training programmes and the absence of long-term follow-up, particularly in the UK. Despite the lack of evaluations, a number of units are employing specific parent-training programmes, as will be seen in the next chapter. There are currently a number of evaluations and research projects ongoing across the country. The major ones are presented here and many of them are using Webster-Stratton's methods of parent-training.

WEBSTER-STRATTON-BASED APPROACHES

SPOKES, London

Since 1991, Webster-Stratton's approach has been employed at the Maudsley Hospital, London. A controlled trial of Webster-Stratton's methods through a community programme is currently underway. The project is called Enabling Parents: Supporting Specific Parenting Skills with a Community Programme (SPOKES) (Scott & Sylva, 1997). This project began in September 1998 and was completed at the end of April 2002. The research is examining interventions to support parents of reception children (aged 4–5 years) in managing child behaviour and learning. The aims of the programme are to provide support to increase parents' ability to manage their children's behaviour, their involvement in constructive pastimes with their children and their involvement with their children's progress at school. Secondary aims are to improve the child's adjustment, by reducing child aggression and antisocial behaviour, and to improve the child's attainments in literacy and attitudes towards reading. Six hundred parents of 5-year-old children at primary schools in inner London were screened. Approximately 120 families will be selected, 60 of whom will be offered both a parent-training package which has been shown to support the parent–child relationship and improve child behaviour and a proven parent support programme to address the child's scholastic difficulties. The remaining parents will receive 'advice only'. Delivery to both groups will be at school. Assessments will take place pre-test, 6–9 months later and one year after the first follow-up.

C'mon Everybody, Sheffield

In 1996 the Sheffield Parenting School was formed. This is the UK's first implementation of the Seattle Parenting Clinic's Parents, Children and Teachers Series programme. Professor Carolyn Webster-Stratton was invited over to train staff in her methods. An annual 'training for trainers' course taught by Carolyn Webster-Stratton is now available in Sheffield. Funding from Sheffield City Council and Sheffield Education Department enabled a small group of Sheffield teachers and social workers to translate their shared concern about the need for parenting education for the parents of young children with behaviour problems into a school-based programme. The project involved running a series of esteem-building courses for primary school children, although they did find that identifying an approach to keep parents engaged proved more difficult. The 12–16-week courses are attended by parents and by children aged 3–4 years, who have been referred through school, health visitors or social services. The intake involves: an assessment process consisting of an initial interview with the family, liaison between parents and schools, telephone support, an evaluation of children's social skills and problem-solving evaluations. The programme's aim is to improve parents' behaviour management, communication skills and play interaction, and children's problem-solving and social skills (Lloyd, 1999). The Home Office funded an evaluation of this work and results were to be published by the end of 1999; we are still awaiting the results.

Other ongoing research

Based at the Health Services Research Unit at the University of Oxford, Patterson *et al* are evaluating a parent-training programme based in primary care. Funded by the NHS Executive South-East, this randomised controlled trial is evaluating the effectiveness of the Webster-Stratton programme delivered in a general practice setting by health visitors who have received particular training. Outcome measures include children's behaviour and maternal anxiety, depression and self-esteem. The children are aged between 2 and 8 years and are registered with one of three Oxford City practices. Initial child behaviour is measured on the Eyberg Child Behaviour Inventory. The authors are expecting to generate data on the level of interest and participation in parenting programmes as well as data on the practicality and effectiveness of running parenting programmes in primary care.

At the Alder Hay Children's Hospital in Liverpool, Professor Jonathan Hill is leading an evaluation of the BASIC programmes as a treatment for low-income families with children diagnosed with conduct disorders.

The BASIC programmes are also being researched alongside the Dinosaur Curriculum for use with high-risk parents and children by the Family Nurturing Network in Oxford.

OTHER APPROACHES

The Parents Plus Programme developed by John Sharry, a social worker at Lucena Clinic, and Dr Carol Fitzpatrick, a consultant psychiatrist at Our Lady's Hospital, Crumlin, Ireland, is an educational package that teaches parents positive ways of preventing and managing misbehaviour in young children (aged 4–11 years). The programme is the first of its kind in Ireland and is thought to represent one of the most powerful and cost-effective ways for professionals to work collaboratively with parents. Video 1 addresses how to communicate positively with children. It shows ways of preventing misbehaviour and positive ways of teaching good social behaviour. The main four sections explore the use of parental attention to change behaviour, play and special time with children, encouragement and praise, and using reward systems effectively. Video 2 looks at a range of skills that parents can use to manage their children's difficult behaviour in as positive a way as possible. The aim of video 2 is to give parents an increased range of options when confronted by their child's misbehaviour, so that they can respond in a calm, confident manner. The video explains how to set rules and help children keep them, how to use active ignoring to reduce misbehaviour, the use of time-out and other sanctions, and how to promote solution building with children. The evaluation of the programme showed that significant gains were made by the treatment group on child behaviour problems, parent–child interaction and parental distress.

The Mellow Parenting programme has been running in the UK since 1990 and is based on the work of NEWPIN. The programme was found to have improved parenting on several dimensions (Puckering *et al*, 1994). Negative interactions as evaluated on videotapes dropped threefold and 80% of the parents involved were able to come off the local child protection register. Although this programme is designed to help parents at risk of abusing a child, it is relevant to the prevention of conduct disorders, as the risk factors for abuse are almost identical to those for conduct disorders. However, as the programme is not aimed specifically at parents of children with conduct disorders the programme is not discussed further within this report.

Based at the Health Services Research Unit at Oxford University, Jane Barlow and Sarah Stewart-Brown are currently conducting a randomised controlled trial of the effectiveness of two parent-training programmes in improving conduct disorders in 3–5-year-old children. Their research, funded by the Medical Research Council, is looking at the effectiveness of two community-based group parent-training programmes. One programme is based on the 'behavioural' model and the other on the 'relationship' model. The control group will receive the standard treatment available for behaviour problems. The groups will be run by trained facilitators skilled in group work and parent-training methods, and will be located in community health centres. The outcome measure will be a behaviour questionnaire to be completed by the parents; the participants will be followed up at six months and one year. The cost-effectiveness and public health benefit of these programmes will also be evaluated.

A project called PEEP is also being examined in the UK. PEEP is an education-focused pre-school project that covers highly disadvantaged areas in Oxford (Buchanan, 1999). 'PEEP aims to build on the growing body of evidence which links such factors as the early development of language, literacy, personal and social development with outcomes relating to higher educational attainment, improved behaviour and crime prevention and the disposition to life-long learning' (PEEP, 1998). Buchanan (1999) explains that among PEEP families 23 different languages are spoken. The project has translated all of the materials it uses and home visits are made to those who find attending groups difficult. A major evaluation is being undertaken at present.

Using the PATHS curriculum (Greenberg *et al*, 1995), which was developed in the US and adapted for use in the Fast Track study, the British experience of Promoting Alternative Thinking Strategies (PATHS) has been found to be effective with deaf children. Currently Flintshire Primary Care Service for Children, Bangor, north Wales, is evaluating PATHS in local schools, as part of a controlled trial designed to assess the impact of a multi-component population-based mental health intervention for young children (Appleton & Hammond-Rowley, 2000).

Home-Start is a network of nearly 200 home-visiting schemes across the UK, supported by a national consultancy. It uses trained volunteers, who are themselves experienced parents, to offer friendship, practical advice and support to families with pre-school children. This network works alongside health and social services and accepts referrals from agencies as well as voluntary organisations. Home-Start works with families for reasons such as domestic violence, suspected child abuse, debt, or children's conduct disorders. Visits by the volunteers usually take place once or twice a week but may be more frequent at certain times. The volunteers share their practical experiences as parents and aim to help parents become more confident in their own abilities in bringing up their children. The Home Office has recently offered Home-Start a grant of £23,000 a year for three years to support two projects in Castleford and Wycombe. Ten other Home-Start projects have received money in grants from the National Lotteries Charity Board (Home Office, 1998). In Buchanan (1999) an evaluation of Home-Start by Frost *et al* (1997) is described. The outcomes of the evaluation are mainly descriptive. Home-Start is seen by families as being non-stigmatising, a complementary service rather than stand-alone and a flexible service. Mothers reported improved well-being and felt they had improved both their informal network and their parenting; however, 43% of mothers did not sustain improvements. Families who do not take part in other programmes seem to take part in these networks; they are often families in transition following a family break-up.

THE COST OF MANUALISED PROGRAMMES

Details of Webster-Stratton programmes and how to order materials can be found on www.incredibleyears.com/. The BASIC series consists of ten videotapes and costs $1300. The ADVANCED series takes an additional 6–19 sessions (an additional six videotapes) and costs an additional $775. Groups usually range from 10 to 14 participants, and one trainer is needed per group. The complete programme includes videotapes, an instructor's manual, and a set of manuals for the participants. Individual programmes cost $175–$245 each.

For the Triple P programme, the items are sold separately. The Group Triple P facilitator's kit is £30. For every parent a basic video and report, *Every Parent's Survival Guide*, is needed, at £40 each, plus a group workbook at £4.40. For more information on the Triple P programme and the products visit www.pfsc.uq.edu.au.

current practice: survey results

Previous chapters have described the difficulties associated with the management and prevention of conduct disorders in young children. Research evidence indicates that parent-training programmes are effective and the elements associated with successful programmes have been presented. It is important from a national policy perspective to ensure that resources are allocated to provide the most appropriate form of treatment. However, we are still waiting for the results of evaluation programmes in practice settings in the UK.

How are services currently addressing the requirement for appropriate management of this group of children? This chapter provides information from a small postal survey that was conducted by FOCUS in August 2000.

One hundred child and adolescent mental health services from around the UK were selected from the FOCUS network database. Every attempt was made to ensure that all regions were included in the survey. A questionnaire was sent to the lead clinician (see Appendix 5 for questionnaire). Sixty-nine questionnaires were returned, of which 67 had been completed – two were returned not completed because the lead clinician no longer worked in that department.

DO ALL SERVICES OFFER PARENT-TRAINING PROGRAMMES?

Of the 67 questionnaires returned, 16 (24%) reported that they did not offer parent-training programmes to parents of young children (under 10 years) with conduct disorders. The reasons given for not offering parent-training programmes included:

- there was insufficient staff time;

- parenting groups were available through local voluntary agencies or health visitors in the area;

- there were unfilled posts or other lack of staff resources;

- it was difficult to set up groups in small rural communities;

- no one at the service was trained in parent-training approaches.

WHAT TYPES OF PARENT-TRAINING PROGRAMMES ARE BEING OFFERED?

Of the 51 services that were offering parent-training programmes, 25 offered two or more types of programme. The types of programmes being offered are represented in Fig. 3.

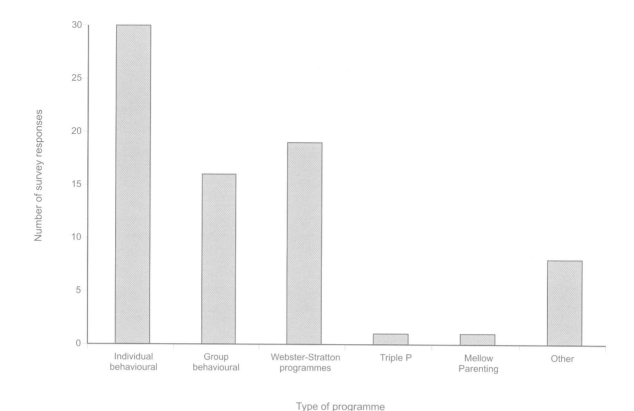

Fig. 3. Types of parent-training programmes offered by survey respondents. Included within the Webster-Stratton programmes are Webster-Stratton-type programmes, Webster-Stratton group and/or videotape programmes and the parent–child game. Included within 'Other' are programmes such as Group-Parent Plus programme, Assertive Parenting by Lee Cantor, Sensory integration group (mainly for ADHD), Russell Barclay Model, cognitive–behavioural therapy group with parallel parent work, and assertive discipline groups.

ARE THE PROGRAMMES EFFECTIVE AND HAVE THEY BEEN FORMALLY EVALUATED?

The majority of survey respondents said they did find the programmes to be effective. Fig. 4 shows the overall responses. Fig. 5 breaks down the responses as to whether the programmes are effective for each type of parent-training programmes.

When asked whether the parent-training programmes had been formally evaluated in their service, 30 out of 48 who responded to this question had not undertaken a formal evaluation and were not planning to do so. Also, when reading the comments, it became apparent that many of the 14 who had responded 'yes' to the question actually meant that they had read about Webster-Stratton's work, which had been evaluated, and therefore had not actually evaluated the work within their service. For this reason the results are somewhat misleading. When asked whether the services had plans to evaluate programmes, despite 21 of 36 responders replying that they did have plans or that it was a possibility that they would, 13 replied 'no'. Two responses did not fit into either category. One felt that these programmes had been researched well in America, with good outcomes, and that parents gave positive feedback, therefore that was enough. Another

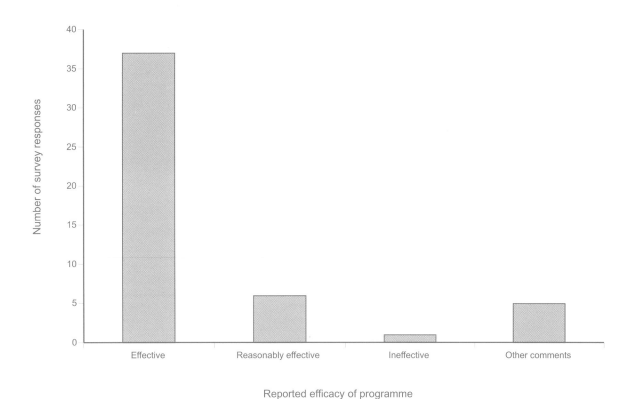

Fig. 4. Survey responses to the question 'Do you find these programmes effective?' 'Other comments' include responses such as: parent-training is still to be established; find parent-training time-consuming.

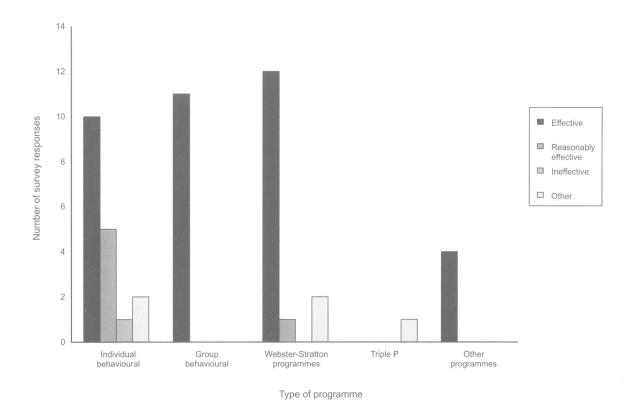

Fig. 5. Reported effectiveness of different types of parent-training programme.

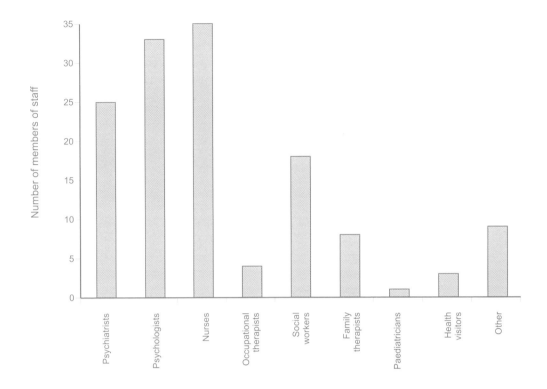

*Fig. 6. Survey responses to the question 'Which staff in your service carry out parent-training programmes?'
'Other' includes: teachers, educational psychologists, primary care workers and a clinical assistant.*

stated that they had no plans to evaluate parent-training programmes specific to conduct disorder but there were plans to evaluate generic parent-training programmes in their service. There were no reasons given for this, although it could be guessed that a lack of staff and resources was probably the most likely reason.

WHICH STAFF ARE CARRYING OUT THE PARENT-TRAINING PROGRAMMES?

When services were asked which of the staff were carrying out the parent-training programmes, the results indicated that many services were involved in multidisciplinary working. The majority responded with a list of different disciplines involved in carrying out the training. A tally was taken of how many members of each profession were involved. The most common combination was a psychiatrist, psychologist and nurses (Fig. 6).

HAVE THESE STAFF BEEN TRAINED IN PARENT-TRAINING TECHNIQUES?

When asked whether many of the staff in these services had been trained in various parent-training techniques, of the 51 responders, 37 replied 'yes'; however, a variety of responses were included for a 'yes', ranging from only the consultant, in the distant past, to all staff are trained in up-to-date techniques. The type and level of training staff had received were also extremely varied. Nineteen of the 33 responses indicated staff had received some kind of training in Webster-Stratton programmes. Within these 19, training varied from courses run in London (at the Maudsley Hospital), Liverpool or Oxford to two teams flying to Seattle in the USA for Webster-Stratton training. Three had had training from Carolyn Webster-Stratton herself, the others by Webster-Stratton teams. The remaining 14 had had training from other sources, which included:

- Mellow Parent training in Leeds and Newcastle;

- Behaviour Management Limited, Bristol;

- 'Getting through the day' group;

- a cognitive–behavioural therapy course;

- in-house training, nothing formal;

- self-training with reference to other packages;

- training in the Triple P programme.

When asked whether their staff would like training, 22 out of 24 replied 'yes'; some services that had indicated that staff had already had some training commented that more training was needed and that they would like new staff to attend courses. A couple of the respondents requested training in evaluated programmes.

WHAT PLANS DO SERVICES HAVE FOR DEVELOPING PARENT-TRAINING PROGRAMMES FURTHER?

Thirty-three out of 51 services answered that they were in the process of or planning to develop parent-training programmes further. Initiatives included:

- plans to start Webster-Stratton children's groups;

- the development of a group for conduct disordered children aged 5–10 years;

- plans to develop a programme of clinical, community-based early-intervention groups;

- the use of a CD–ROM interactive programme, 'Parenting Wisely';

- the development of Webster-Stratton programmes to complement community programmes;

- efforts to obtain funding for new staff.

The reasons given by a few services that responded negatively to developing parent-training programmes included:

- 'tried to set up parenting groups in schools, attendance was poor, may try again';

- 'intend to if we can attract funding and create a demand';

- 'pessimistic about Webster-Stratton group, trying to work out ways to use the programme more successfully'.

Reasons for having no plans to develop parent-training programmes (10 services) included:

- 'believe that this is a Social Service or Education issue';

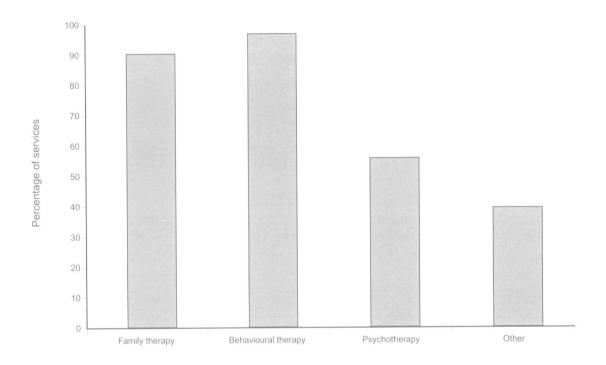

Fig. 7. Percentage of services offering treatments other than parent-training to children with conduct disorders. 'Other' includes: cognitive–behaviour therapy, social skill training, play therapy, music/art therapy, medication if ADHD was also present, school liaison, multi-agency 'system' and holistic interventions, and routine occupational therapy.

- 'not a top priority';
- 'no plans at present but may consider it in the future'.

WHAT OTHER INTERVENTIONS ARE BEING OFFERED TO THESE CHILDREN IN THESE SERVICES?

As well as parent-training programmes, the questionnaires asked about what other interventions were offered to young children with conduct disorders in these services. Most of the sample responded that they offered more than one type of treatment. Most offered behavioural and family therapy. Psychotherapy was offered by just over half of the services (Fig. 7).

WHO REFERS THESE CHILDREN TO CHILD AND ADOLESCENT MENTAL HEALTH SERVICES?

The final question asked the services to estimate how many referrals to child and adolescent mental health services came from which professional group. For those that answered this question, the majority of referrals came from general practitioners, followed by social services, the education authority and then paediatricians. Other referrals came from health visitors, school nurses, speech and language therapists, parents, or the police. The high number of referrals from general practitioners were accounted for in some cases by responses including:

- 'referrals have to have GP approval';

- 'referrals from GPs only except for exceptional cases';

- 'some CAMHS services don't take referral from education, education told to go through GP';

- 'social services non-existent in our area'.

After examining all the responses by region, there were no differences between regions on any of the questions. The provision of parent-training programmes seems to be evenly distributed throughout the UK. It would appear that behavioural programmes, individual and group programmes, are the most widely used. Webster-Stratton's programmes are also being used throughout the UK and this type of programme and other group behavioural programmes appear to be the most effective, according to many clinicians. Nonetheless, it is apparent that many services have not evaluated these programmes within their services, though many are planning to do so. Training of staff in parenting programmes also varies throughout the UK, with just over a third requesting further training.

summary of key issues

As conduct disorders are the most common problems being referred to child and adolescent mental health services, it is important to increase the implementation of effective intervention programmes. Most of the evaluations of parent-training programmes have been in the United States and Australia, and to date little evaluation has been conducted in the UK; this is changing. It seems that making parent-training programmes accessible via the community and schools decreases stigmatisation of the children and increases the parents' involvement in the programmes. Webster-Stratton's approaches are, at present, the most documented and most evaluated; it will be interesting to see the findings of the evaluations of these programmes that are currently underway in the UK.

A number of issues highlighted in this report need to be considered for future research and practice. The quality of the research included in this report has been discussed in Chapter 2.

LIMITATIONS OF CURRENT RESEARCH

- There is little information regarding differences in girls' and boys' responses to treatment and as a result no information is available to guide decisions about specific treatment matches for girls with conduct disorders.

- More follow-up studies are needed to ascertain whether improved behaviour is maintained over time. In particular, studies need to examine the relationship between the initial severity of the problems or the duration of the programme and the maintenance of effects over time.

- Long-term outcomes of parent-training programmes need to consider the extent to which changes in children's behaviour is carried over to other settings, such as the school, and which parents benefit from which 'type' of parent-training programme.

- More research is needed to test the effectiveness of programmes in clinical practice as opposed to trials conducted in universities with volunteer families.

- More research is needed to examine whether dealing with parental problems such as depression and marital conflict before or during parent-training programmes increases the effectiveness of the programmes.

- More research is needed to investigate methods to increase parent enrolment and sustained participation in parent-training programmes.

- More information is needed on the cost-effectiveness of all types of intervention and how to decide on the optimum mix of programmes, as some include manuals and videotapes and therefore are expensive.

KEY FINDINGS

- Parent-training programmes are effective in decreasing conduct disorders in young children.

- Behavioural parent-training programmes, both individual and group programmes, are the most effective in reducing conduct disorders in young children.

- Group parent-training programmes are more cost-effective than individual parent-training programmes and provide the parents with peer support.

- It would appear that the duration of many of the current programmes (10–20 weeks) may well be too short and that programmes should be sustained for more severe problems.

- Research suggests that the pre-school age may be one of the most critical times developmentally at which to prevent the onset of conduct disorders.

diagnostic criteria for conduct disorder and oppositional defiant disorder (DSM–IV and ICD–10)

DSM–IV DIAGNOSTIC CRITERIA FOR CONDUCT DISORDER (American Psychiatric Association, 2000)

A. A repetitive and persistent pattern of behavior in which the basic rights of others or major age-appropriate societal norms or rules are violated, as manifested by the presence of at least three (or more) of the following criteria in the past 12 months, with at least one criterion present in the past six months.

Aggression to people and animals

1   often bullies, threatens or intimidates others

2   often initiates physical fights

3   has used a weapon that can cause serious physical harm to others (e.g., a bat, brick, broken bottle, knife, gun)

4   has been physically cruel to people

5   has been physically cruel to animals

6   has stolen while confronting a victim (e.g., mugging, purse snatching, extortion, armed robbery)

7   has forced someone into sexual activity

Destruction of property

8   has deliberately engaged in fire setting with the intention of causing serious damage

9   has deliberately destroyed others' property (other than by fire setting)

Deceitfulness or theft

10 has broken into someone else's house, building or car

11 often lies to obtain goods or favors or to avoid obligations (i.e., 'cons' others)

12 has stolen items of nontrivial value without confronting a victim (e.g., shoplifting, but without breaking and entering; forgery)

Serious violations of rules

13 often stays out at night despite parental prohibitions, beginning before age 13 years

14 has run away from home overnight at least twice while living in parental or parental surrogate home (or once without returning for a lengthy period)

15 is often truant from school, beginning before age 13 years

B. The disturbance in behaviour causes clinically significant impairment in social, academic, or occupational functioning.

C. If the individual is age 18 years or older, criteria are not met for Antisocial Personality Disorder.

Type based on age of onset:

Childhood-Onset Type: onset of at least one criterion characteristic of Conduct Disorder prior to age 10 years.

Adolescent-Onset Type: absence of any criteria characteristic of Conduct Disorder prior to age 10 years.

Unspecified Onset: age at onset is not known

Specify severity:

Mild: few if any conduct problems in excess of those required to make diagnosis *and* conduct problems cause only minor harm to others

Moderate: number of conduct problems and effect on others intermediate between 'mild' and 'severe'

Severe: many conduct problems in excess of those required to make the diagnosis *or* conduct problems cause considerable harm to others

DSM–IV DIAGNOSTIC CRITERIA FOR OPPOSITIONAL DEFIANT DISORDER (American Psychiatric Association, 2000)

A. A pattern of negativistic, hostile and defiant behavior lasting at least 6 months, during which four or more of the following are present:

1 often loses temper

2 often argues with adults

3 often actively defies or refuses to comply with adults' requests or rules

4 often deliberately annoys people

5 often blames others for his or her mistakes or misbehavior

6 is often touchy or easily annoyed by others

7 is often angry and resentful

8 is often spiteful or vindictive

Note: Consider a criterion met only if the behavior occurs more frequently than is typically observed in individuals of comparable age and developmental level.

B. The disturbance in behavior causes clinically significant impairment in social, academic or occupational functioning.

C. The behaviors do not occur exclusively during the course of a Psychotic or Mood Disorder.

D. Criteria are not met for Conduct Disorder, and, if the individual is age 18 years or older, criteria are not met for Antisocial Personality Disorder.

(Reprinted with permission from the *Diagnostic and Statistical Manual of Mental Disorders*, 4th edn, text revision. Copyright 2000 American Psychiatric Association.)

ICD–10 DIAGNOSTIC CRITERIA FOR CONDUCT DISORDERS (World Health Organization, 1992)

F91 Conduct disorders

Conduct disorders are characterised by a repetitive and persistent pattern of dissocial, aggressive, or defiant conduct. Such behaviour, when at its most extreme for the individual, should amount to major violations of age-appropriate social expectations, and is therefore more severe than ordinary childish mischief or adolescent rebelliousness. Isolated dissocial or criminal acts are not in themselves grounds for the diagnosis, which implies an enduring pattern of behaviour.

Disorders of conduct may in some cases proceed to dissocial personality disorder. Conduct disorder is frequently associated with adverse psychosocial environments, including unsatisfactory family relationships and failure at school, and is more commonly noted in boys. Its distinction from emotional disorder is well validated; its separation from hyperactivity is less clear and there is often overlap.

Judgements concerning the presence of conduct disorder should take into account the child's developmental level.

Examples of the behaviours on which the diagnosis is based include the following: excessive levels of fighting or bullying; cruelty to animals or other people; severe destructiveness to property; fire-setting; stealing; repeated lying; truancy from school and running away from home; unusually frequent and severe temper tantrums; defiant provocative behaviour; and persistent severe disobedience. Any one of these categories, if marked, is sufficient for the diagnosis, but isolated dissocial acts are not.

Exclusion criteria include uncommon but serious underlying conditions such as schizophrenia, mania, pervasive developmental disorder, hyperkinetic disorder and depression. Conduct disorder overlaps with other conditions. The coexistence of emotional disorders of childhood should lead to a diagnosis of mixed disorder of conduct and emotions. If a case meets the criteria for hyperkinetic disorder, that condition should be diagnosed instead. Milder or more situational-specific levels of overactivity and inattentiveness are common in children with conduct disorder, as are low self-esteem and minor emotional upsets; neither excludes the diagnosis.

F91.0 Conduct disorder confined to the family context

This category comprises conduct disorders involving dissocial or aggressive behaviour in which the abnormal behaviour is almost entirely confined to the home and/or interactions with members of the household. Diagnosis requires that there be no significant conduct disturbance outside the family setting and that the child's social relationships outside the family be within normal range. It is possible that these highly situation-specific conduct disorders do not carry the generally poor prognosis associated with pervasive conduct disturbances.

F91.1 Unsocialized conduct disorder

This type of conduct disorder is characterised by the combination of persistent dissocial or aggressive behaviour, with a significant pervasive abnormality in the individual's relationships with other children. The lack of effective integration into a peer group constitutes the key distinction from 'socialised' conduct disorders. Often isolated from or rejected by other children, they have a lack of reciprocal relationships with others in the same age group. Relationships with adults tend to be marked by discord, hostility and resentment. Often there is some associated emotional disturbance.

Offending is often solitary. Typical behaviours include: bullying, excessive fighting, excessive levels of disobedience, rudeness, uncooperativeness and resistance to authority, severe temper tantrums and uncontrolled rages, destructiveness to property, fire-setting and cruelty to animals and other children. The nature of the offence is therefore less important in making the diagnosis than the quality of personal relationships. The disorder is pervasive across situations and may be most evident at school; specificity to situations other than the home is compatible with the diagnosis.

F91.2 Socialized conduct disorder

The key differentiating feature is the presence of long lasting friendships with others of the same age. Often the peer group will consist of other youngsters involved in delinquent activities, but the child's dissocial behaviour may take place away from a non-delinquent peer group. If the behaviour involves bullying, there may be disturbed relationships with victims or some other children. Relationships with adults in authority tend to be poor. Emotional disturbances are minimal. The disorder is most evident outside the family context and often the school or other out of home settings are compatible with the diagnosis.

F91.3 Oppositional defiant disorder

In ICD–10 ODD is considered to be a subtype of conduct disorders. ODD usually becomes evident before the age of 9 or 10 years. It is defined by the presence of markedly defiant, disobedient, provocative behaviour, which is clearly outside the normal range of behaviour for a child of the same age in the same sociocultural context, and which does not include the more serious violations of the rights of others as reflected in the aggressive and dissocial behaviour specified for categories F91.0 and F91.2. Children with this disorder tend to defy adult requests or rule and deliberately annoy others. They usually tend to be angry, resentful and easily annoyed by other people whom they blame for their own mistakes or difficulties. Typically their defiance has a provocative quality, so that they initiate confrontations and generally exhibit excessive levels of rudeness, uncooperativeness and resistance to authority.

This behaviour is often most evident in interactions with adults or peers whom the child knows well. The key distinction from other types of conduct disorder is the absence of behaviour that violates the law and the basic rights of others, such as theft, cruelty, bullying, assault and destructiveness.

(Reprinted with permission from the *ICD–10 Classification of Mental and Behavioural Disorders: Clinical Descriptions and Diagnostic Guidelines*. Copyright 1992 World Health Organization.)

search strategies and filters used in literature search

SEARCH 1 ADHD AND DISRUPTIVE BEHAVIOUR DISORDERS

No.	Request
1	explode "psychotherapy"/all subheadings
2	explode "family-relations"/all subheadings
3	parent*
4	family*
5	father*
6	mother*
7	paternal*
8	maternal*
9	couple*
10	marital*
11	psycho*
12	therap*
13	psycho* near1 therap*
14	behavio*
15	therap*
16	behavio* near5 therap*
17	behavio*
18	intervention*
19	behavio* near5 intervention*
20	behavio*
21	treatment*
22	behavio* near5 treatment*
23	multimodal*
24	multi-modal*
25	MTA
26	#1 or #2 or #4 or #5 or #6 or #7 or #8 or #9 or #10 or #13 or #16 or #19 or #22 or #23 or #24 or #25
27	#3 and #26
28	explode "Attention-Deficit-and-Disruptive-Behavior-Disorders"/all subheadings
29	child*
30	#28 and #29
31	#27 and #30

SEARCH 2 BEHAVIOURAL PROBLEMS

1	explode "psychotherapy"/all subheadings
2	explode "family-relations"/all subheadings
3	parent*
4	family*
5	father*
6	mother*
7	paternal*
8	maternal*
9	couple*
10	marital*
11	psycho*
12	therap*
13	psycho* near1 therap*
14	behavio*
15	therap*
16	behavio* near5 therap*
17	behavio*
18	intervention*
19	behavio* near5 intervention*
20	behavio*
21	treatment*
22	behavio* near5 treatment*
23	multimodal*
24	multi-modal*
25	MTA
26	#1 or #2 or #4 or #5 or #6 or #7 or #8 or #9 or #10 or #13 or #16 or #19 or #22 or #23 or #24 or #25
27	#3 and #26
28	behavio*next
29	problem*
30	behavio*next problem*
31	behavio*
32	problem*
33	behavio*
34	problem*
35	behavio* near1 problem*
36	difficult
37	behavio*
38	difficult near1 behavio*
39	#35 or #38
40	child*
41	#39 and #40
42	#27 and #41

Filter for systematic review and meta-analyses

43	TG=ANIMAL
44	TG=HUMAN
45	TG=ANIMAL
46	(TG=ANIMAL) not ((TG=HUMAN) and (TG=ANIMAL))
47	#42 not #46
48	REVIEW-ACADEMIC in PT
49	REVIEW-TUTORIAL in PT
50	META-ANALYSIS in PT
51	META-ANALYSIS
52	SYSTEMATIC*
53	REVIEW*
54	SYSTEMATIC* near REVIEW*
55	SYSTEMATIC*
56	OVERVIEW*
57	SYSTEMATIC* near OVERVIEW*
58	META-ANALY*
59	METAANALY*
60	META
61	ANALY*
62	META-ANALY* or METAANALY* or (META ANALY*)
63	#62 in TI
64	#62 in AB
65	#47 or #49 or #50 or #51 or #54 or #57 or #62 or #64
66	#48 or #49 or #50 or #51 or #54 or #57 or #62 or #64
67	#47 and #66

Filter for randomised controlled trials

43	TG=ANIMAL
44	TG=HUMAN
45	TG=ANIMAL
46	(TG=ANIMAL) not ((TG=HUMAN) and (TG=ANIMAL))
47	#42 not #46
48	RANDOMIZED-CONTROLLED-TRIAL in PT
49	CONTROLLED-CLINICAL-TRIAL in PT
50	RANDOMISED-CONTROLLED-TRIALS
51	RANDOMI*ED-CONTROLLED-TRIAL*
52	RANDOM-ALLOCATION
53	DOUBLE-BLIND-METHOD
54	SINGLE-BLIND-METHOD
55	CLINICAL-TRIAL in PT
56	explode CLINICAL-TRIALS/all SUBHEADINGS
57	clin*near

58	trial*
59	clin*
60	trial*
61	(clin* near trial*) in TI
62	clin*
63	trial*
64	(clin* near trial*) in AB
65	singl*
66	doubl*
67	trebl*
68	tripl*
69	blind*
70	mask*
71	(singl* or doubl* or trebl* or tripl*) near (blind* or mask*)
72	(#71 in TI) or (#71 in AB)
73	PLACEBOS
74	placebo*
75	placebo* in TI
76	placebo*
77	placebo* in AB
78	random*
79	random* in TI
80	random*
81	random* in AB
82	RESEARCH-DESIGN
83	TG=COMPARATIVE-STUDY
84	"Evaluation-Studies"
85	explode "Evaluation-Studies"/all subheadings
86	FOLLOW-UP-STUDIES
87	PROSPECTIVE-STUDIES
88	control* or prospectiv* or volunteer*
89	(#88 in TI) or (#88 in AB)
90	#48 or #49 or #51 or #52 or #53 or #54
91	#55 or #56 or #61 or #64 or #72 or #73 or #75 or #77 or #79 or #81 or #82
92	#83 or #85 or #86 or #87 or #89
93	#90 or #91 or #92
94	#47 and #93

Abbreviations for outcome measures used in Appendix 3.

ADAS	Abbreviated Dyadic Adjustment Scale
BAAQ	Brief Anger Aggression Questionnaire
BCS	Behavioural Coding System
BDI	Beck Depression Inventory
CAPI	Child Abuse Potential Inventory
CBCL	Child Behaviour Checklist
CES–D	Center for Epidemiological Studies Depression Scale
CII	Coder Impression Inventory
CSQ	Client Satisfaction Questionnaire
DAS	Dyadic Adjustment Scale
DASS	Depression Anxiety Stress Scale
DDI	Daily Discipline Interview
DPICS	Dyadic Parent–Child Interaction Coding System
DPICS-R	Dyadic Parent–Child Interaction Coding System – Revised
DRS	Diagnostic Reading Scale
ECBI	Eyberg Child Behaviour Inventory
FOS-R-III	Revised Family Observation Schedule
HIWC	Home Inventory with Child
IEE	Interview of Emotional Experience
INVOLVE	Parent–Teacher Involvement Questionnaire
IRS	Interaction Rating Scale
LES	Life Experiences Survey
MAT	Parents Completed Marital Adjustment Test
MESSY	Matson Evaluation of Social Skills with Youngsters
PBQ	Preschool Behaviour Questionnaire
PCIT	Parent–Child Interaction Task
PDR	Parent Daily Report
PPC	Parent Problem Checklist
PPS-I CARE	The Peer Problem-Solving-Interaction Communication-Affect Rating Coding System
PS	Parenting Scale
PSI	Parenting Stress Index
PS-I CARE	Problem-Solving-Interaction Communication-Affect Rating-Engagement System
PSOC	Parenting Sense of Competency Scale
SHP	Social Health Profile
SPST-R	Child Social Problem-Solving Test – Revised
TOCA-R	Teacher Observation of Classroom Adaptation – Revised
TRF	Achenbach Teacher Report Form
WALLY	Wally Child Social Problem-Solving Detective Game

PAPERS APPRAISED IN THIS REPORT

Systematic reviews

Reference	Studies included	Population	Interventions	Results	Follow-up
Brestan & Eyberg (1998)	Eighty-two studies were included. They were all reported in articles published between 1966 and 1995. This review included all ages of children and adolescents.	Studies included: 3917 boys; 883 girls; 472 children of unspecified sex. In the 26 studies reporting children's mean age, overall mean = 9.89 years (SD = 3.98).	The studies included were all prospective studies of psychosocial treatments in which a measured goal of the intervention was to decrease conduct problem behaviour.	Two 'well established' treatments were identified. They were: parent-training based on *Living with Children* (Patterson & Guillion, 1968) – operant principles of behaviour change for older children and adolescents with conduct disorders; and videotape modelling parent-training (Webster-Stratton's programme). Ten other treatments were found to have empirical support to be 'probably efficacious treatments'.	The availability of six-month follow-up data was one of the criteria used in assessing the studies.
Barlow (1999)[a]	Three meta-analyses and 18 randomised controlled trials, two of which were follow-up studies. Studies were all reported in papers published between 1970 and 1997.	Children between the ages of 3 and 10 years with behavioural problems.	Different types of group-based parent-training programmes were included, but only those which directly focused on work with parents.	The behavioural-type programmes were extremely effective in improving behaviour problems in children. Although Adlerian and PET programmes were effective in bringing about a change in behaviour, they were not as effective as the behavioural programmes. Community-based programmes appeared to produce better changes in children's behaviour.	Long-term follow-up to assess whether behaviours were maintained over time ranged from six months to three years. None of the studies provided evidence concerning the relationship between the initial severity of the problems or the duration of the programme and effects over time.

[a]This systematic review included summary tables for the critical appraisal of the meta-analyses and the randomised controlled trials, which are reproduced in Appendix 5.

*Additional randomised controlled trials, 1990–2000
(not appraised in previous systematic reviews)*

Treatment of conduct disorders

Reference	Patients	Intervention	Outcome measures	Results	Follow-up
Webster-Stratton (1994)	Eighty-five families of children aged 3–8 entered the study; descriptive data of 78 families who completed the study are given. Seventy-five per cent of subjects were boys, 25% were girls. All children were referred by parents and met DSM-III criteria for ODD/CD or both. Children were excluded if they had a physical impairment, intellectual deficit or history of psychosis. No data on on ethnic breakdown are given.	After families had completed BASIC group discussion videotape modelling (GDVM), 39 families were assigned to no further treatment and 38 to the ADVANCE group. ADVANCE meant parents came to the clinic weekly for 14 additional two-hour sessions. The sessions covered areas such as personal self-control, communication skills, problem-solving skills between adults, teaching children to problem solve and and strengthening social support and self-care.	Parents completed: MAT; BAAQ; BDI; PSI; CBCL; ECBI; and a consumer questionnaire. Children were scored on SPST-R. Observers completed DPICS and PS-I CARE.	Both groups reported significant reductions in behaviour post-GDVM ($P < 0.001$) and home observations noted a significant reduction in child non-compliance post-GDVM ($P < 0.001$). ADVANCE produced improvements in parents' communication, problem-solving skills and consumer satisfaction. ADVANCE mothers reported more improvements in adjustment than GDVM-only mothers ($P < 0.01$). Children in the ADVANCE programme showed an increase in knowledge of pro-social solutions ($P < 0.01$). ADVANCE did not enhance improvements in child behaviour.	No long-term follow-up was carried out.

Reference	Patients	Intervention	Outcome measures	Results	Follow-up
Webster-Stratton & Hammond (1997)	Ninety-seven children aged 4–7 years (mean 5.7 years); 74% boys, 85.6% Caucasian. All children were referred by parents and met DSM–III criteria for ODD or CD or both. All children with ODD and ADHD were included in the trial. Children were excluded if they had a physical impairment, intellectual deficit or history of psychosis.	Children and families were assigned to four groups: waiting-list control (CON) (n = 22); parent-training (PT) (n = 26); child-training (CT) (n = 27); parent- and child-training (PT+CT) (n = 22). The CON group waited 9 months and were then allocated to one of the three programmes. The CT programme included videotaped vignettes and fantasy play that addressed interpersonal difficulties. The PT programme included videotaped programmes on parenting and interpersonal skills. PT+CT included both but were held separately.	Parents were measured on: ECBI; CBCL; PSI; PDR and a consumer satisfaction questionnaire. Teachers were measured on PBQ. Observers used DPICS-R; PS-I CARE and PPS-I CARE. Children were assessed on WALLY.	Of mothers in the PT group, 81% reported improvements in child's behaviour. Of mothers in the CT+PT group, 70% reported improvement, compared with 27% in the CON group (P < 0.01). CT did not differ significantly from the CON group. All three groups differed from the CON group in reduction of child negative behaviour reported by mothers (P < 0.001). A reduction in criticism from mothers of 30% or more occurred to the greatest extent in the CT+PT group and the PT group compared with CON (P < 0.05). CT did not differ from CON. Observers saw no significant differences in reduction of behaviour between treatment and CON conditions.	At one-year follow-up, the proportion of children who achieved a reduction of at least 30% in deviant behaviour was 73.7% CT, 60% PT and 95% CT+PT. There was no CON group to compare with at one-year follow-up.
Taylor et al (1998)	One hundred and eight families with children between 3 and 8 years old entered study. Eighty of the families had a boy as the identified child. All parents reported English was the language most spoken at home.	Families were not assigned randomly to groups. Forty-six families were assigned to Webster-Stratton's Parentand Child Series (PACS), whereby parents took part in the BASIC parenting groups. Forty-six	Parents were measured on: ECBI; CBCL; PDR; DAS; BAAQ; Therapy Attitude Inventory. Teachers were asked to complete TRF. Children were evaluated on MESSY.	Design of the study meant comparisons could not be done simultaneously. Mothers in the PACS group reported fewer problems on ECBI intensity (P < 0.01) andECBI problem score (P < 0.05) compared with those in the waiting-list group. Mothers in the eclectic treatment	No long-term follow-up was carried out.

	Sample	Method	Outcome measures	Results
	All children were referred by parents and were assessed using ECBI. No mention is made of co-morbidity.	families were assigned to an eclectic treatment condition in which they were offered the approach to treatment typically offered at the centre. Eighteen families were assigned to a waiting-list group.		group reported fewer problems on mother's ECBIproblem score ($P < 0.05$) comparedwith the waiting-list group. The PACSgroup reported fewer problems on the ECBI score than mothers in the eclectic treatment group ($P < 0.05$).
Sanders et al (2000)	Three hundred and five families took part in the study. Sixty-eight per cent of children were boys. No figures on ethnic groups, but mainly Caucasian. The child had to be aged between 36 to 48 months; mothers had to rate behaviour as being in the elevated range of ECBI; no developmental disorder or significant health impairment. They had to have a problem such as depression or low income and not be receiving psychological help at the time.	Families were divided into enhanced behavioural family intervention (EBFI) ($n = 58$), standard behavioural family intervention (SBFI) ($n = 65$), self-directed behavioural family intervention (SDBFI) ($n = 61$) and waiting-list (WL) ($n = 71$) groups. The WL families received no treatment. The SDBFI group received a 10-session self-directed programme, comprising two workbooks. The SBFI group were taught the same strategies as in the SDBFI sessions. Parents attended 10 one-hour sessions given by a trained practitioner. The EBFI parents received the same as the SBFI group as well as partner support and coping skills. Parents attended approximately 12 appointments (totalling 14 hours).	Outcome measures included observation of mother and child behaviour coded using FOS-R-III. Parent report measures were: BDI; CAPI; ECBI; PDR; PS; PSOC; PPC; ADAS; DASS; CSQ.	After assessment, children in EBFI showed significantly less observed negative behaviour than children in SDBFI and WL conditions ($P < 0.05$). Mothers in EBFI reported significantly fewer child behaviour problems on the PDR at post-intervention compared with all other conditions. Mothers in the SBFI condition reported less child problem behaviour than those in the WL condition ($P < 0.001$). Authors found a greater proportion of children in the EBFI condition showed significant change at post-intervention when compared with children in the WL and SDBFI groups. More children in SBFI showed a 30% reduction in negative behaviour than in the SDBFI condition. No significant differences at follow-up between conditions, although improvements in observed negative child behaviour achieved pre- to post-intervention were maintained for the EBFI and SBFI conditions.

Prevention of conduct disorders

Reference	Patients	Intervention	Outcome measures	Results	Follow-up
Webster-Stratton (1998)	Four hundred and twenty-six families completed baseline assessments to begin trial. Children were 4 years old (mean = 56.53 months); 53% were boys. Thirty-seven per cent of the children represented minority groups. Subjects came from nine Head Start centres, with families enrolling children. Children were at high risk of ODD or CD or both.	The nine Head Start centres were assigned to either the experimental condition (PARTNERS) or the regular centre-based Head Start programme (control). Of the 394 who completed post-assessment, 264 were in PARTNERS and took part in 8 or 9 weekly parent group meetings. Parents viewed videotapes of modelled parenting skills. Topics included how to play with your child, using praise and encouragement, and how to give and get support. The 130 families in the control group attended services provided by a Head Start centre. There was no real control group in the study.	Parents completed: Discipline Style and Techniques question-naire; DDI; INVOLVE; CBCL; ECBI; Family Demographic Interview. Depression: CES-D; Parent Past History; BAAQ; LES. Independent observers completed: DPICS-R; CII for the home and child. Teachers completed INVOLVE and TRF.	Mothers in PARTNERS increased their discipline competence, positive affect, praise and physical positive behaviours (P < 0.001). The control mothers showed no changes on observed parenting behaviours. Intervention teachers reported increases in parental involvement with their children's education and contact with school compared with control mothers. Intervention children decreased their deviant and non-compliant behaviours (P < 0.001), increased their positive affect (P < 0.01) and increased their social competence according to teacher reports, where as control children remained stable over time. Independent observations of child behaviours indicated 73% of the high-risk children showed at least a 30% reduction in negative and no compliant behaviours at home compared with 55% of high-risk control children (P < 0.05).	At one-year follow-up, the differences between the groups for the high-risk mothers' reductions in criticisms were no longer significant. Differences between groups for children's behaviour were also non-significant. Children still had significant increases in their levels of positive affect and decreases in their negative affect with their mothers at home.

Reid et al (1999)	Of 671 children taken from 12 schools, 51% were female and 87.4% were European American. Ethnicity and other demographic information was collected for mothers, fathers and the child. Children were seen as 'at risk' of developing ODD/ CD or both due to the catchment areas of the schools in which they lived.	Two schools (382 children) were in the multi-modal preventive intervention condition. Two schools (289 children) in the control condition and two in the intervention condition were chosen as alternatives if and when a school in the study dropped out. One school from each of these groups was then assigned to either first-graders or fifth-graders. Multi-modal intervention included: a school component, which comprised 20 1-hour sessions over 10 weeks aiming to decrease aggressive behaviour and improve peer interactions. The parent component consisted of parents meeting in groups each week for six weeks, when they were taught how to create a home environment most conducive to ongoing practice of good discipline and supervision.	No specific outcome measures are listed other than the Walker–McConnell Scale of Social Competence and School Adjustment. Researchers report that outcome measures included family assessment (focusing on child behaviour problems), academic skills, peer relations and family management skills.	Social skills in the intervention group viewed more favourably ($P < 0.05$) by their teachers the following year than in the control group. Mothers with highest levels of aversive verbal behaviour changed more ($P < 0.05$) in the intervention group than in the control group. At post-assessment children in the intervention group averaged 4.8 aversive behaviours per 30 minutes in the playground compared with 6.6 in the control group (no significance level given).	Post-assessment was taken one year later. No follow-up data available yet.

Reference	Patients	Intervention	Outcome measures	Results	Follow-up
Conduct Problems Prevention Research Group (1999a)	Of the 891 children included in the study (mean age 6.5 years, SD 0.48 years), 69% were male, 51% were African American, 47% were European American and 2% were of other ethnicity. These children came from 54 schools within four areas. In the total sample (see next paper) there were 7560 children. All children were living in areas regarded as 'high-risk' for the development of ODD, CD or both. These 891 were identified as being behaviourally disruptive at kindergarten and had general behaviour problems.	The schools were randomly assigned to the intervention (445 children in 191 classrooms) or control conditions (446 children in 210 classrooms). All children received the PATHS curriculum throughout the year in classrooms (see next paper). The 891 children (high-risk sample) were offered parent groups, child social skills training groups and academic tutoring during a weekly 2-hour programme held at the school on Saturdays or weekday evenings over 6 months. In addition, weekly home visits or telephone contact was made with the families between sessions.	Many outcome measures were used: Emotion Recognition Questionnaire; IEE; Social Problem-Solving Measure; HIWC; Woodcock-Johnson Psych-Educational Battery – Revised; DRS; Social Competence Scale – Parent Form; SHP; Parent Questionnaire; Parent–Teacher Involvement Questionnaire – Parent; Parent–Teacher Involvement Questionnaire – Teacher; developmental history; ratings of parent change; Parent Satisfaction Questionnaire; CBCL; PDR; TRF; TOCA-R; PCIT; BCS; IRS; CII.	The intervention group improved on emotional recognition ($P < 0.0001$), emotion coping ($P < 0.05$) and social problem solving ($P < 0.01$), and decreased on laggressive retaliation ($P < 0.05$) compared with the control group. The intervention group had more positive peer interaction ($P < 0.05$) and higher social peer preferences ($P < 0.05$) than the control group. The intervention group parents rated their change in parenting satisfaction more positively ($P < 0.05$) than control parents. Behaviour change ratings from parents and teachers showed more improvement in the intervention group ($P < 0.001$) than in control children. Changes on other measures of behaviour were moderate.	No long-term follow-up data are available.

Conduct Problems Prevention Research Group (1999b)	Approximately 48 schools in 'high-risk' neighbourhoods were used in the study. There were 7560 children in total, all in in grade 1. Without including the high-risk children in the previous paper, the sample size in this analysis is 6715. The percentage of ethnic minority children in each school and other demographic data are reported.	Schools for each area were divided into matched sets and then randomly assigned. There were 198 intervention classrooms and 180 control classrooms. Those children in the intervention classrooms were taught the Fast Track version of the PATHS curriculum. Forty per cent of lessons focused on skills related to understanding and communicating emotions; 30% focused on skills related to the increase of positive social behaviour; and 30% focused on self-control and other steps in social problem solving. Teachers were encouraged to generalise their use of PATHS concepts to other settings, including the home.	Outcomes were derived from three sources. Teachers completed TOCA-R and SHP and were interviewed about the behaviour of each child in their class. Peer reports of aggression and likeability were measured using sociometric interviews. Observers assessed the quality of the classroom atmosphere.

Observers rated the intervention classrooms as having a more positive atmosphere. Children in the intervention classrooms were found to be better at following rules ($P < 0.05$) and expressing feelings appropriately ($P < 0.05$). The classroom level of interest and and enthusiasm ($P < 0.01$) and ability to stay focused on a task ($P < 0.005$) was higher in intervention than in the control group.

The project is continuing to teach PATHS through to to grade 5. No follow-up data are available at present.

APPRAISAL OF SYSTEMATIC REVIEWS

Brestan & Eyberg (1998)

Assessment of the review

The question the review sets out to answer is clearly focused, although not particularly specific. All psychosocial interventions, including parent-training programmes, for the treatment of conduct problems, including conduct disorder and oppositional defiant disorder, are reviewed. The population is both children and adolescents with conduct problems. The outcome measured is a decrease in behaviour problems. Studies are included if the treatment was applied to children with comorbid diagnoses that explicitly included conduct problems. Treatments for substance misuse are not included.

The authors examined papers from 1966 to 1995. Studies before 1993 were taken from four meta-analyses examining the same issue and from empirically validated treatments from *Clinical Psychologist*, which had periodically published empirically validated treatment lists and literature. For studies between 1993 and 1995 literature searches were carried out. No mention of which databases were searched appears in the text, although the journals that were hand searched are mentioned individually by name. The authors included only studies that were published in a peer-reviewed journal.

Quality of the studies

Every study was assessed to determine whether it met the 'Chambless criteria' for 'well established treatments' and 'probably efficacious treatments'. The authors selected four minimal criteria for good design: use of a comparison group, use of reliable measures, use of random assignments to groups, and a report of attrition rates. Seven other criteria were also used in coding the studies: 12 or more participants per group or 25 or more participants per group, use of blind assessment, use of a treatment manual, reports of six-month follow-up data, reports of descriptive statistics and reports of treatment integrity data.

Results

This review covers children of all ages. For the purpose of this report only information of relevance to young children with conduct disorder has been reported.

The authors identified two treatments that were 'well established': parent-training programmes based on *Living with Children* (Patterson & Guillion, 1968) and videotape modelling (Webster-Stratton, 1984). The authors also identified ten treatments as being 'probably efficacious' for the treatment of conduct disorders in both young children and adolescents. Of the ten, those relating to younger children incorporated the following treatment strategies: parent–child treatments based on Hanf's (1969) two-stage behavioural treatment model for pre-school children (Peed *et al*, 1977; Zangwill, 1983; Hamilton & MacQuiddy, 1984; Wells & Egan, 1988; McNeil *et al*, 1991; Eyberg *et al*, 1995) and the delinquency prevention programme (Tremblay *et al*, 1995).

Conclusions

Two studies used interventions that met the criteria for 'well established' treatment conditions: videotape modelling parent-training and parent-training programmes based on *Living with Children*. Brestan & Eyberg note that the numbers of children in the studies varied tremendously and there was a lack of demographic details included in most of the papers reviewed. The review also included a number of older studies, which were reported as having insufficient data and being less well designed.

Barlow (1999)

Assessment of the review

The question that the review sets out to answer is clearly focused. Group-based parent-training programmes are reviewed. The population is children aged 3 to 10 years with behavioural problems. Improvement in the child's behaviour according to parents' reports and independent observations was the outcome measure.

The literature search is thorough. The years covered are 1970 to 1997. The author lists the databases that were used and the 'grey literature' that was searched. The search terms are described well. Only published studies are included; the author is aware that this could have led to publication bias.

Assessment of the studies

The author reviewed three meta-analyses (Cedar & Levant, 1990; Todres & Bunston, 1993; Serketich & Dumas, 1996) and 18 randomised controlled trials, including two follow-up studies. The three meta-analyses and 16 of the randomised controlled trials (not the two follow-up studies) are assessed thoroughly. The quality of these studies is presented in appendix 5 of this report.

Results

The three meta-analyses

The findings of the three meta-analyses indicate that 'behavioural parent-training programmes in particular are effective in modifying children's behaviour as measured by a combination of both parent report outcome measures and independent observations of children's behaviour'. The results suggest that the Adlerian and PET programmes are both less effective than the behavioural programmes in modifying children's behaviour. For the separate results of the meta-analyses see pages 13–17 of Barlow's review.

The 16 randomised controlled trials

A number of outcome measures were used to assess treatment effects, including parents' reports of behaviour and independent observations. Owing to the heterogeneity of these studies, results from each included study are presented separately (see pages 21–36 of Barlow's review). Overall, the findings suggest that 'group-based parent-training programmes were effective in terms of both parent-report and independent observations of children's behaviour, and that the behavioural programmes produced the best results'.

Conclusions and comments

'The results of both the meta-analyses and randomised controlled trials were similar, pointing to the effectiveness of behaviourally-orientated parent-training programmes, in improving behaviour problems in children. The results indicated that the Adlerian and PET type programmes were effective but to a lesser extent than the behavioural programmes'. It appeared that community-based group programmes may produce better changes in children's behaviour and be more cost-effective than individual clinic-based programmes. The author notes the many methodological problems with the research and the lack of long-term follow-up. There was also less rigorous research available on the effectiveness of the relationship programmes.

CRITICAL APPRAISAL OF RANDOMISED CONTROLLED TRIALS (TREATMENT STUDIES)

Webster-Stratton (1994)

Are the results of this trial valid?

Was the group of patients clearly defined? (Consider: the population studied, comorbidity, classification used, outcomes measured)

Eighty-five families were entered in the study. The families had children, aged 3–8 years, with conduct disorders; 75% of children were boys, 25% girls. All children had severe conduct disorders as rated by parents, and if the children met DSM–III criteria for ODD, CD or both, they were included in the study. Children were excluded if they had a physical impairment, intellectual deficit or a history of psychosis.

Outcome measures: Parents completed the MAT, BAAQ, BDI, PSI, CBCL, ECBI and a consumer satisfaction questionnaire. Children were scored on the SPST-R. Observers completed the DPICS and PS-I CARE.

Was the assignment of patients to treatments randomised? Was the randomisation list concealed?

All parents attended the basic group discussion videotape modelling (GDVM) training programme, presented as 12 or 13 two-hour sessions weekly at the clinic.

After the basic (GDVM) programme, 39/40 families were randomly assigned to no further treatment and 38 families to the ADVANCE group.

It was impossible to conceal the list from clinicians as the intervention was treatment or no treatment.

Were all patients who entered the trial accounted for at its conclusion?

The author tells us that 6 families did not complete the basic GDVM training and 1 family did not complete the ADVANCE training. Therefore 78 families completed the study.

No significant differences existed between the groups.

Were they analysed in the groups to which they were randomised?

No mention is made as to whether the families who did not complete training are included in the analysis.

Were patients and clinicians kept 'blind' to which treatment was being received?

It is unclear as to whether the parents knew they had been split into two groups. Assessors who observed behaviours were unaware of hypotheses of study.

Aside from the experimental treatment, were the groups treated equally?

The no-treatment group did not attend any more sessions after basic GDVM, as the author felt it unethical for the no-treatment group to attend 14 further sessions which would not provide treatment. The number of assessment contacts, however, was kept constant across the two conditions.

What are the results?

Both groups reported significant ($P < 0.001$) reductions in behaviour problems on the ECBI and CBCL post-GDVM and home observations noted a significant reduction in child non-compliance in the short-term immediately following GVDM ($P < 0.001$).

ADVANCE produced additional significant improvements in parents' communication and problem-solving skills on PS-I CARE and in consumer satisfaction. ADVANCE mothers reported significantly ($P < 0.01$) more improvements in adjustment than GDVM-only mothers.

From the SPST-R, children in the ADVANCE programme showed significant increased knowledge of pro-social solutions ($P < 0.01$).

What are the implications of this paper for local practice?

Are the results of this study generalisable to your patients? (Does your patient resemble those in the study? What are your patient's preferences? Are there alternative treatments available?)

Details of demographic variables on the families are given; however, no details on ethnic background are given, therefore no comment is made as to whether any differences in the programme's results are caused by cultural problems.

The programme could be easily used elsewhere, as therapists in the study use a manual and videotapes.

Parents seemed to be very satisfied with the programme.

Additional comments

ADVANCE did not enhance improvements in child behaviour. The author suggests a ceiling effect is occurring due to the GDVM treatment that all families had received beforehand. No control group was used in this study to investigate this further.

The author also notes that long-term follow-up assessments are necessary to determine possible delayed effects on children's behaviour as a result of parents' improved communication, problem-solving and coping skills.

Webster-Stratton & Hammond (1997)

This paper is discussed in detail by Cunningham (1998).

Are the results of this trial valid?

Was the group of patients clearly defined? (Consider: the population studied, comorbidity, classification used, outcomes measured)

Ninety-seven children between the ages of 4 and 8 years (according to the abstract) or 4 and 7 years (according to the method section) referred by parents with conduct disorders and meeting DSM–III criteria for ODD, CD or both were included in the study; 74% were boys, 26% girls; and 85.6% were Caucasian children. All children with ODD and ADHD were included in the trial because, the authors explain, of the high comorbidity of these problems. Children were excluded if they had a physical impairment, intellectual deficit or a history of psychosis.

Outcomes measured: Parent report measures of child behaviour were assessed using the ECBI, CBCL, PSI, PDR and a consumer satisfaction questionnaire. Teacher reports of child's behaviour were measured using the PBQ. Independent observations of child and parent interaction were measured on DPICS-R, PS-I CARE and PPS-I CARE. Assessments of child's social problem solving was measured using WALLY.

Was the assignment of patients to treatments randomised? (Was the randomisation list concealed?)

Children and families were randomly assigned to four groups: waiting-list control ($n = 22$); parent-training (PT) ($n = 26$); child-training (CT) ($n = 27$); and child- and parent-training (CT+PT) ($n = 22$).

It was impossible to conceal the randomisation list from the clinicians.

Were all patients who entered the trial accounted for at its conclusion?

At one-year follow-up, three families in the CT group refused to participate. All other groups had 100% participation rates.

Were they analysed in the groups to which they were randomised?

The authors note that one child in the CT group did not complete training but they point out that the family was included in the analysis. It is not clear whether the three who refused to participate were analysed in the groups to which they were assigned.

Were patients and clinicians kept 'blind' to which treatment was being received?

It was impossible to keep clinicians and parents blind to the treatment groups. However, the 8 home observers assessing parent–child interaction were not informed of treatment conditions and the 6 trained observers assessing parent problem solving were not informed of the hypothesis of the study.

Aside from the experimental treatment, were the groups treated equally?

The control group received no treatment and had no contact with therapists. The children in the CT group came to the clinic weekly for 22 two-hour sessions. The parents in the PT group met weekly in groups for two-hour sessions over 22–24 sessions. The CT+PT group were identical to the above programmes but were held separately.

If a cross-over design is used, are attempts made to reduce the carry-over effects? (Did the authors acknowledge that this was a potential problem?)

The authors note that it was difficult to determine whether the long-term changes were due to maturation or to treatment, as after nine months the control group were reassigned to one of the three training groups. Therefore at one-year follow-up, there was no control group to assess.

What are the results?

Eighty-one per cent of mothers in PT group reported improvements in their child's behaviour on CBCL, and 70% of mothers in the CT+PT group reported improvement compared with 27% control group ($P < 0.01$). Child-training did not differ significantly from the control group. All three treatment groups differed significantly from the control group in the reduction of child negative behaviour as reported by mothers on PDR ($P < 0.001$).

The independent observers noted that a reduction of more than 30% in criticism from mothers occurred to the greatest extent in the CT+PT group (71%) and the PT group (68%), which was significantly different from control mothers ($P < 0.05$). Again, child-training did not differ significantly from the control group. The results from the independent observers for behaviours showed that, although the reduction of negative behaviours was greater for the treatment conditions compared with the control group, this was not significant.

At one-year follow-up, the percentage of children who achieved a reduction of at least 30% in deviant behaviour was 73.7% CT, 60% PT and 95% for CT+PT, as reported by the independent observers.

What are the implications of this paper for local practice?

Are the results of this study generalisable to your patients? (Does your patient resemble those in the study? What are your patient's preferences? Are there alternative treatments available?)

This appears to be an affordable and logistically feasible programme. Treatment manuals and videotapes allow this programme to be disseminated to other settings. Consumer satisfaction with the programmes was high: 92.6% of CT mothers, 90% of CT fathers and 95% of PT and CT+PT mothers and fathers reported 'positive' to 'very positive' improvements in children's behaviour as a result of the training programme.

Additional comments

As the authors point out, in parent-training programmes many parents do not attend and 30–50% of children do not improve after parent-training; therefore, child-training in addition may be appropriate. As the child-training is taught in schools, it could help to decrease behaviour problems in the school environment. Child-training, being a group programme, is also cost-effective.

Taylor et al *(1998)*

Are the results of this trial valid?

Was the group of patients clearly defined? (Consider: the population studied, comorbidity, classification used, outcomes measured)

There were 108 families with children between the ages of 3 and 8 years, with conduct disorders. Eighty of the families participating had a boy as the identified child. All parents reported that English was the language most spoken at home. There is no mention of comorbidity.

All children were assessed using the ECBI.

Outcome measures: Parents were asked to complete the ECBI, CBCL, PDR (by telephone), BDI, DAS, Support Scale, BAAQ and Therapy Attitude Inventory. Teachers were asked to complete the TRF and children were evaluated on the MESSY.

Was the assignment of patients to treatments randomised? (Was the randomisation list concealed?)

The assignment of patients was not randomised, as before randomisation the population was split in to two groups, 'urgent' and 'non-urgent'. The urgent group were randomly assigned to either of the treatment groups. The non-urgent group were randomly assigned to either the waiting-list group or a treatment group. Forty-six families were assigned to the Parent and Child Series (PACS), 46 participated in the eclectic treatment and 18 families were assigned to the waiting-list.

Please note that 110 families were assigned to one of the three groups; however, the authors state at the beginning of the study that only 108 families took part.

It was impossible to conceal the randomisation list from clinicians and patients.

Were all patients who entered the trial accounted for at its conclusion?

All patients are accounted for. The authors tell us that eight families dropped out of the eclectic treatment group and five families dropped out of the PACS group.

Were they analysed in the groups to which they were randomised?

Post-test data were collected, if possible, on the families that dropped out. An intention-to-treat analyses is performed.

Were patients and clinicians kept 'blind' to which treatment was being received?

As mentioned before, clinicians and patients were not blind, but research assistants were not informed of treatment assignment. However, some of the patients told the research assistants when they came to collect follow-up data what group they were in.

Aside from the experimental treatment, were the groups treated equally?

The PACS therapists were more highly skilled than the therapists carrying out eclectic treatment. Therapists carrying out eclectic treatment had some knowledge of PACS, which was hard to control for. The PACS treatment consisted of group work, the eclectic intervention of individual treatment, and it was therefore also hard to control for this confounding factor. No mention is given as to what interaction the control group had with therapists.

What are the results?

The design of the study did not allow comparisons to be done simultaneously in a single analysis, as the waiting-list group was comparable to only a subsample of each of the two treatment groups.

Mothers in the PACS treatment group reported significantly fewer problems on ECBI intensity ($P < 0.01$) and ECBI problem score ($P < 0.05$) than those in the waiting-list group. Mothers in the eclectic treatment group reported significant differences on ECBI problem score ($P < 0.05$) compared with the waiting-list group.

The PACS group reported significantly fewer problems on the ECBI problem score ($P < 0.05$) than mothers in the eclectic treatment group, and higher levels of consumer satisfaction ($P < 0.01$) than those in eclectic treatment group. Of the PACs group, 41% continued to report problems in ECBI range, compared with 74% of parents in the eclectic group.

What are the implications of this paper for local practice?

Are the results of this study generalisable to your patients? (Does your patient resemble those in the study? What are your patient's preferences? Are there alternative treatments available?)

This is one of the few studies that has taken a research-based treatment and used it in a clinical setting. It has been shown that a manualised approach can be used in a clinical setting with good results. The programme was found to be effective and cost-effective.

Parents reported that, after being in a PACS group, they were more confident. Eighty per cent of the PACS group found training good or very good, compared with 50% in the eclectic treatment group.

Unfortunately, families were not randomised properly to the groups, and therefore the results should be treated with caution.

Additional comments

It was found that, in reality, children had less severe conduct problems than found in Webster-Stratton's research studies.

Authors note shortcomings of the project, including the small numbers studied, the fact that direct observations were not included, missing data, that fact that follow-up was only short-term and that there was limited information regarding eclectic treatment programmes.

Parents were informed that they would be paid $30 to complete post-test data and $50 to complete same questionnaires one year later.

Sanders et al *(2000)*

Are the results of this trial valid?

Was the group of patients clearly defined? (Consider: the population studied, comorbidity, classification used, outcomes measured)

Participants were 305 families with a three-year-old child. The parents responded to a community outreach campaign targeted at three low-income areas of Brisbane.

The family had to meet the following criteria to take part in the study. The child had to be between 36 and 48 months of age. The mothers had to rate their child's behaviour as being in the elevated range on the ECBI. The child had to show no evidence of a developmental disorder or significant health impairment and not already be receiving help for behavioural problems. The parents had to meet at least one of the following criteria: maternal depression, relationship conflict, single-parent household, low gross family income or low occupational prestige, no current therapy for psychological problems and not intellectually disabled.

Sixty-eight per cent of children were boys and the parents were predominantly Caucasian.

Outcome measures: These included observation of mother and child behaviour coded using the FOS-R-III. Parent report measures were the BDI, CAPI, ECBI, PDR, PS, PSOC, PPC, ADAS, DASS and CSQ.

Was the assignment of patients to treatments randomised? (Was the randomisation list concealed?)

It is unclear how the families were randomised. The authors simply state that a randomised group comparison design was used with four conditions: level 5 enhanced Triple P (EBFI), level 4 standard Triple P (SBFI), level 4 self-help Triple P (SDBFI) and waiting-list control (WL). Neither is it clear how many families were assigned to each condition. The authors point out that there were no significant differences across conditions on any measure at pre-intervention, which indicates that the samples of families in each group were comparable.

It was impossible to keep the randomisation list concealed from parents and clinicians owing to the nature of the intervention.

Were all patients who entered the trial accounted for at its conclusion?

All families were accounted for at the end of the trial. There were no significant differences in completion rates versus non-completion rates across the conditions. The authors examine the possibility of differential attrition, and mothers with higher ratings of negative affect were less likely to complete post-assessment in the EBFI condition. Across all four conditions, mothers who did not complete intervention rated their child's behaviour as more problematic than those who did complete the programme.

At one-year follow-up, there were no significant differences in the rate of completion across the three conditions, although a significant main effect for mother's ratings of negative affect was found, with higher ratings among those who did not complete the intervention. Mother's ratings of their child's behaviour were found to affect completion of the programme, with higher ratings of negative behaviour for those who did not complete it.

Were they analysed in the groups to which they were randomised?

This is unclear.

Were patients and clinicians kept 'blind' to which treatment was being received?

The 12 clinicians trained and supervised in the interventions were not aware of the conditions the families had been assigned to before the pre-intervention assessment.

All of the coders coding the videotaped observations were blind to the intervention conditions of the participants, the stage of assessment, the interactions used for reliability checks, and the specific hypotheses being tested.

Aside from the experimental treatment, were the groups treated equally?

Families allocated to the SDBFI condition were given the self-directed materials and instructed how to use them. Families allocated to the practitioner-assisted conditions (EBFI and SBFI) attended 60–90-minute weekly sessions with a practitioner on an individual basis in local community health centres. The intervention families were reassessed following the completion of the intervention and then reassessed one year after the programme was completed. Families allocated to the WL condition received no treatment and had no contact with the research team for 15 weeks. At one-year follow-up, there was no WL group for comparison, as this group, after the post-intervention assessment, participated in the programme of their choice and took no further part in the study.

What are the results?

At post-intervention, children in the EBFI condition showed significantly less observed negative behaviour on the FOS-R-III than children in SDBFI and WL conditions ($P < 0.05$).

Mothers in the EBFI condition reported less negative child behaviour on the ECBI than mothers in the SDBFI and WL conditions at post-intervention, and mothers in the SBFI condition reported less negative behaviour than those in the WL condition ($P < 0.001$).

Mothers in the EBFI condition also reported less negative child behaviour on the PDR compared with mothers in the SDBFI, WL and SBFI conditions ($P < 0.01$, $P < 0.001$, $P < 0.05$ respectively) at post-intervention. Mothers in the SBFI condition also reported less negative child behaviour problems on the PDR than mothers in the SDBFI, who in turn reported fewer child behaviour problems than mothers in WL condition. Fathers followed the same pattern of results.

At post-intervention, both mothers and fathers in the EBFI and SBFI conditions reported less frequent use of dysfunctional discipline strategies on PS than parents in the WL condition. Mothers and fathers also reported less use of dysfunctional discipline than parents in the SDBFI condition.

Mothers in the EBFI and SBFI conditions reported greater competence on PSOC than mothers in the SDBFI and WL conditions.

Using 30% reduction criteria, the authors found that a greater proportion of children in the EBFI condition showed significant change on ECBI at post-intervention when compared with children in the WL and SDBFI conditions. Significantly more children in the SBFI showed a 30% reduction in negative behaviour than in the SDBFI condition.

The authors also found a significantly greater proportion of children whose behaviour on the ECBI had moved from the clinical to the non-clinical range in the EBFI, SBFI and SDBFI conditions when compared with the WL condition. More children in the EBFI condition moved into the non-clinical range than in the SBFI condition at post-intervention.

At one-year, the percentage of intervals of child negative behaviour on ECBI and PDR decreased significantly in the SDBFI condition only. Although the improvements in observed negative child behaviour achieved pre- to post-intervention were maintained for the EBFI and SBFI conditions, there were no significant differences at follow-up between conditions on this measure.

What are the implications of this paper for local practice?

Are the results of this study generalisable to your patients? (Does your patient resemble those in the study? What are your patient's preferences? Are there alternative treatments available?)

The authors note that the findings cannot be generalised to all settings as the study used a media outreach strategy to recruit the sample.

The WL group could not be compared at one-year follow-up, although the authors discuss this.

All parents were satisfied with the programme they received, although parents who participated in the practitioner-assisted programmes (EBFI and SBFI) reported significantly higher levels of consumer satisfaction than parents in the self-directed programme.

Additional comments

All intervention conditions (EBFI, SBFI and SDBFI, in that order) were superior to the WL control condition in the short term in improving child's behaviour. The enhanced condition also produced the most consistent short-term changes on measures of parenting practices and competence, followed by the standard and self-directed programmes.

Long term, however, the enhanced condition did not produce any superior outcomes on measures of parental adjustment or parenting. It is argued that EBFI may not have been sufficiently intensive; however, this would have increased the drop-out rate and the cost.

The authors suggest that there may be little benefit in offering parents generic enhanced interventions that target parental distress and that perhaps services should offer specific additional modules to those families who require it following an initial trial of SBFI.

There is a need to consider the higher level of attrition among families with more severe child behaviour problems and higher levels of maternal depression and marital conflict.

CRITICAL APPRAISAL OF RANDOMISED CONTROLLED TRIALS (PREVENTION STUDIES)

Webster-Stratton (1998)

Are the results of this trial valid?

Was the group of patients clearly defined? (Consider: the population studied, comorbidity, classification used, outcomes measured)

Subjects came from nine Head Start centres, with families enrolling with children at high risk of ODD, CD or both. Of the 542 families who enrolled, 426 completed baseline assessments to begin the trial. Children were aged 4 years (mean = 56.53 months, SD 4.26.); 53% were boys, 47% girls. Of the subjects, 17% were African American, 6% Hispanic, 4% Asian American, 4% Native American and 6% a combination. Descriptions of parents and background are given.

No mention is made of comorbidity or classification, as children were not diagnosed with a disorder but rather as being at high risk of developing conduct disorders.

The major domains to be measured were parenting competencies, child social competencies, and parental involvement in schools; ratings were made by parents, teachers and independent observers.

Outcome measures: Parents completed the DDI; INVOLVE; Social Competence Scale – Parent; CBCL; ECBI; Family Demographic Interview, Depression; parent past history; BAAQ; and LES.

Independent observers completed independent observations in the home (DPICS-R and CII) of parenting style; and independent observations of the child in the home (again, DPICS-R and CII).

Teachers completed INVOLVE; Social Competence Scale – Teacher Reports (T-COMP); TRF.

Was the assignment of patients to treatments randomised? (Was the randomisation list concealed?)

The nine Head Start centres (64 classes) were randomly assigned, by lottery, to either the experimental condition, in which parents, teachers and family service workers (FSWs) participated in the intervention (PARTNERS) or the control condition, in which parents, teachers and FSWs participated in the regular centred-based Head Start programme.

Were all patients who entered the trial accounted for at its conclusion?

At post-assessment the number of families had dropped from 426 to 394. The authors state that there where no significant differences between the groups in terms of those who had dropped out.

Were they analysed in the groups to which they were randomised?

The 394 who completed post-intervention assessments were analysed regardless of the 'dosage' of intervention that they had received; 264 were in intervention group, 130 were in the control group.

Were patients and clinicians kept 'blind' to which treatment was being received?

It was obvious to patients and clinicians which group they were in. Observers were unaware of the groups the children and families were in and were assigned to observe equal numbers from the two conditions.

Aside from the experimental treatment, were the groups treated equally?

The number of assessment contacts and procedures were identical for the two groups.

If a cross-over design is used, are attempts made to reduce the carry-over effects? (Did the authors acknowledge that this was a potential problem?)

There were more families in the intervention group than in the control group, as families that during the first year had been in the control group became part of the intervention group. The authors were aware that this was a problem.

What are the results?

Intervention mothers significantly ($P < 0.001$) increased their discipline competence, positive affect, praise and physical positive behaviours, and significantly decreased their harsh or critical behaviour commands and negative affect. The control mothers showed no changes on observed parenting behaviours.

Intervention teachers using INVOLVE reported significant increases in parents' involvement with their children's education ($P < 0.01$) and contact with school ($P < 0.05$), compared with the control group.

Intervention children significantly ($P < 0.001$) decreased their deviant and non-compliant behaviours, negative misbehaviour and poor conduct, whereas the control children remained stable over time on these variables of the DPICS-R. They significantly ($P < 0.01$) increased in positive affect, whereas the control children remained unchanged on DPICS-R. They significantly increased their social competence according to teacher reports, but the control children did not change.

From the DPICS-R and CII, 69% of high-risk mothers in the intervention condition showed a 30% reduction in critical statements compared with 52% of the high-risk mothers in the control condition at post-assessment ($P < 0.05$). Independent observations of child behaviours indicated 73% of the high-risk intervention children showed at least a 30% reduction in negative and non-compliant behaviours at home compared with 55% of high-risk control children ($P < 0.05$).

When examining high-risk mothers at one-year follow-up, the difference between the groups for the high-risk mothers' reductions in criticisms was no longer significant. The difference between groups for the high-risk children's behaviour was also non-significant.

Children from the intervention condition one year later still had significant increases in their levels of positive affect ($P < 0.01$) and decreases in negative affect ($P < 0.01$) in their interactions with their mothers at home compared with control children on DPICS-R.

What are the implications of this paper for local practice?

Are the results of this study generalisable to your patients? (Does your patient resemble those in the study? (What are your patient's preferences? Are there alternative treatments available?)

The author notes that Head Start attracts the most motivated among poor families and this may have biased the results.

The drop-out rate, once parents started the programme, was low – only 17% did not attend at least 50% of the sessions.

Consumer satisfaction with the programme was high and 92% of participants reported that they would recommend the programme to other parents. The majority of parents (79%) wanted their groups to continue.

Additional comments

The author notes that it may have been advantageous to have had a third comparison group of families who were matched according to low income and other demographic and risk factors but who were not enrolled on Head Start as, Head Start provided support services and parent classes also.

The author also notes that the base rate of problem behaviours was low to begin with, which would have made it difficult to detect group differences.

At the one-year follow-up, lack of funds meant that only a subsample of teachers could make the teacher report assessments: only 34% of the intervention children and 35% of the control children were reassessed by teachers.

The author gives an interesting footnote. When the data were analysed separately for the parent completers, those who attended more than 50% of the parent sessions offered showed significant reductions in the use of physically negative discipline approaches and increased positive affect compared with the control mothers.

Reid et al *(1999)*

Are the results of this trial valid?

Was the group of patients clearly defined? (Consider: the population studied, comorbidity, classification used, outcomes measured)

Children and their families living in at-risk neighbourhoods were studied. 'At-risk' areas were judged according to the percentage of households in the schools' catchment area with at least one juvenile detainment. Children were taken from 12 schools within these areas, and were from grades 1 or 5 only. The final sample included 671 children, of whom 51% were female. There were 382 in the intervention schools and 289 in the control schools. Of the families, 87.4% were European American.

Comorbidity and classification are not mentioned, as children were not diagnosed just at high-risk of developing ODD, CD or both.

Outcome measures: These included family assessment, which focused on child behaviour problems, academic skills, peer relations and family management skills. For each of the areas, information was collected from multiple agents (teachers, parents, children staff), using multiple methods (interviews, questionnaires, observations), in multiple settings (school, home, laboratory). The only measure listed is the Walker–McConnell Scale of Social Competence and School Adjustment.

Was the assignment of patients to treatments randomised? (Was the randomisation list concealed?)

Schools were drawn out of a hat. Two schools were drawn for the multi-modal preventive intervention condition, two schools as controls, and two as alternatives. One school from each of these three groups was then randomly assigned as a first-grade school and the other as a fifth-grade school.

Were all patients who entered the trial accounted for at its conclusion?

Over the course of the project, one school chose not to participate and two schools dropped out of the pool. It is unclear as to what effect this had on the results.

The percentage of missing data regarding the children and parents is given and possible reasons for this is discussed.

The number of subjects included in the final analyses is not clear.

Were they analysed in the groups to which they were randomised?

The authors do not mention whether children who dropped out were analysed in the groups to which they were randomised.

Were patients and clinicians kept 'blind' to which treatment was being received?

Staff members conducting observations were kept blind as to who were in the intervention group. Teachers' perceptions taken the following year were carried out by new teachers to the children.

Aside from the experimental treatment, were the groups treated equally?

The groups were not treated equally, as the control schools were given $2000 for participation in the study. What the schools did with the money is listed: one school spent money on a similar programme to LIFT, which therefore compromised the trial.

What are the results?

Individual data are not given, and some data are presented in graph form. Only regression weights and effect sizes for outcome analyses are provided.

Social skills of children in the intervention group were viewed more favourably ($P < 0.05$) by their teachers the following year than those of children in the control group.

Mothers with the highest levels of aversive verbal behaviour changed the most ($P < 0.05$) in the intervention group compared with the control group.

Before intervention, playground observations revealed that youngsters in the control and intervention schools averaged approximately 0.2 aversive physical behaviours per minute (6 per 30 minutes). Following intervention, children in the experimental and control conditions averaged 4.8 and 6.6 aversive behaviours per 30 minutes, respectively (no significance level is given).

The authors note that the effect sizes for outcome analyses range from small to large in magnitude; the strongest effects were for the most distressed children and mothers, as indexed by the pre-intervention score.

What are the implications of this paper for local practice?

Are the results of this study generalisable to your patients? (Does your patient resemble those in the study? What are your patient's preferences? Are there alternative treatments available?)

The parent programme was received well by participants: 94% said that they would recommend the programme to other parents. The most popular components in the programme were those on discipline strategies, setting effective limits, making a connection with school and establishing home study routines.

Teachers were also satisfied with the programme, with 100% of first-grade teachers recommending the programme to other teachers.

Many schools dropped out of the study, and the reasons for this are examined. One of the schools that had to be included in the study was below the median of households with at least one juvenile detainment.

Conduct Problems Prevention Research Group (1999a)

Are the results of this trial valid?

Was the group of patients clearly defined? (Consider: the population studied, comorbidity, classification used, outcomes measured)

Fifty-four schools within four areas took part in the study. The schools were selected as high risk on the basis of crime and poverty statistics of the neighbourhoods they served. Behaviourally disruptive kindergarten children were identified and screened from the schools, and the top 10% on a number of screening measures were included in study. These 891 children (in grade 1) had a mean age of 6.5 years (SD 0.48); 69% of them were male, 31% female. Fifty-one per cent of the sample was African American, 47% European American and 2% 'other' ethnicity.

Comorbidity is not mentioned as these children were at high risk for ODD, CD or both and had general behaviour problems.

Outcome measures: A number of measures were used to generate a score. The top 10% were seen as 'high risk' and included in the study. Measures included teacher observations, TOCA-R and CBCL.

Many outcome measures were used. For the child's social cognition and reading the tools used were: the Emotion Recognition Questionnaire; IEE; Social Problem-Solving Measure; HIWC; Woodcock–Johnson Psych-Educational Battery – Revised; DRS. For the child's peer relations and social competence, assessments were made using: Social Competence Scale – Parent Form; teachers' ratings were collected using the SHP and peer nominations were collected. Parenting behaviour and social cognition were assessed using: Parent Questionnaire; INVOLVE (parent and teacher forms); developmental history; ratings of parent change; and a Parent Satisfaction Questionnaire. Observational assessment of parenting and child behaviour on the PCIT used the BCS, IRS and CII. The child's aggressive/disruptive behaviour was assessed using the CBCL and PDR. Teachers' ratings were collected using the TRF and TOCA-R. Parental satisfaction with the intervention was also recorded.

Was the assignment of patients to treatments randomised? (Was the randomisation list concealed?)

Entire schools were randomly assigned to the intervention or control condition. All selected children in grade 1 were consequently in the intervention group (445 children in 191 classrooms) or control group (446 children in 210 classrooms), depending on which school they attended.

Were all patients who entered the trial accounted for at its conclusion?

Yes.

Were they analysed in the groups to which they were randomised?

Regardless of the extent to which families engaged in interventions, they were taken into account in all analyses reported, if their child was in regular education placement in an intervention school in mid-November of the grade 1 year.

Were patients and clinicians kept 'blind' to which treatment was being received?

It was impossible to keep them blind.

Parents were paid $15 for every session attended.

Observers were unaware of the experimental conditions within schools, but it is unclear whether they were aware of which group parents were assigned to on the home visits.

Aside from the experimental treatment, were the groups treated equally?

The control families were not contacted throughout the first year.

What are the results?

The intervention group improved its mean scores across time in emotional recognition ($P < 0.0001$), emotion coping ($P < 0.05$) and social problem solving ($P < 0.01$) and decreased its mean score for aggressive retaliation ($P < 0.05$) significantly more than did the control group. Corresponding effect sizes were given as 0.54, 0.25, 0.33 and 0.23. The intervention group spent more time in positive peer interaction than did the control group ($P < 0.05$), and received higher peer social preference scores ($P < 0.05$), with effect sizes given as 0.27 and 0.28, respectively. The intervention group reported less use of physical punishment in response to hypothetical vignettes after grade 1 than the control group ($P < 0.05$) (effect size = 0.23).

Teachers rated the parent involvement in school as greater for the intervention group than for the control group.

Parents in the intervention group rated their change in parenting satisfaction and ease of parenting more positively than did those in the control group ($P < 0.05$) (effect size = 0.33).

Behaviour change ratings from both parents and teachers revealed more behavioural improvement among children in the intervention group than in the control group ($P < 0.001$) (effect sizes = 0.50 and 0.53, respectively).

Other effect sizes for behaviour change were moderate but not significant.

The mean number of minutes of special education decreased significantly for the intervention group compared with control group ($P < 0.05$) (effect size = 0.26).

What are the implications of this paper for local practice?

Are the results of this study generalisable to your patients? (Does your patient resemble those in the study? What are your patient's preferences? Are there alternative treatments available?)

Parents reported high levels of satisfaction with the overall helpfulness of Fast Track, with the family-based components, the child-focused group, tutoring and the PATHS curriculum.

Additional comments

This appears to be a costly programme. There is little evidence that it decreased conduct problems. The authors remind the reader that the study was looking at 10% of children with the worst behaviour problems in neighbourhoods that had substantial economic deprivation, crime and delinquency. The authors suggest that the first-year results demonstrate the potential for adapting intervention components originally developed in clinic settings and making them suitable for preventive efforts targeting high-risk populations.

Poorly participating families were not dropped from the study; instead, they were tracked carefully to allow for future investigations in examining participation in interventions.

Conduct Problems Prevention Research Group (1999b)

Are the results of this trial valid?

Was the group of patients clearly defined? (Consider: the population studied, comorbidity, classification used, outcomes measured)

Approximately 48 schools in 'high-risk' neighbourhoods were selected from four areas in the US. High-risk status was defined from estimated rates of delinquency and juvenile arrest in the neighbourhoods.

There were 198 intervention classrooms and 180 comparison classrooms over three cohorts. Of the 7560 children in these classrooms, 845 were deemed as at high-risk for ODD, CD or both (these children are described in more detail in the previous paper). Therefore sample size for analyses that do not include the high-risk children is 6715. All children were in grade 1.

Comorbidity is not relevant in this study as these children had not been diagnosed with a disorder.

Outcomes measures: These were derived from three sources. Teachers completed the TOCA-R and SHP, and were interviewed regarding the behaviour of each child in their class. Using sociometric interviews, peer reports of aggression and likeability were obtained. Observers assessed the classroom 'atmosphere'.

Was the assignment of patients to treatments randomised? (Was the randomisation list concealed?)

Schools from each area were divided into matched sets, which were then randomly assigned to 198 intervention classrooms and 180 control classrooms.

It was impossible to conceal the randomisation from teachers, parents and children, because of the nature of the intervention.

Were all patients who entered the trial accounted for at its conclusion?

The sample size may be presumed to be 6715 throughout, although no mention of the numbers analysed are given in the results section.

Were they analysed in the groups to which they were randomised?

This is not discussed.

Were patients and clinicians kept 'blind' to which treatment was being received?

It was impossible to blind parents and teachers. Observers were unaware of the status of the school and therefore unbiased.

Aside from the experimental treatment, were the groups treated equally?

Although the number of ratings per class was dependent on the number of 'high-risk' children in a particular classroom, there was no difference in the number of times intervention versus control classrooms were rated.

What are the results?

High-risk children were also receiving other treatment, as they were part of a larger study. Therefore analyses were done twice – with and without the high-risk group.

The data presented excludes the high-risk children, and are therefore more conservative.

In peer interviews, intervention classrooms had lower aggression scores than did the control classrooms. For prosocial behaviour and 'most liked' ratings, the effect of the intervention was not significant.

Observers rated intervention classrooms as having a more positive classroom atmosphere. There were significant findings favouring the intervention group over the comparison group in terms of children's ability to follow rules ($P < 0.05$), ability to express feelings appropriately ($P < 0.05$), the classroom level of interest and enthusiasm ($P < 0.01$) and the classroom's ability to stay focused and on task ($P < 0.005$).

For both the intervention and control groups, teachers who taught more cohorts had higher classroom atmosphere ratings. Also, ratings of teacher skill in programme implementation and classroom management predicted positive programme outcomes.

What are the implications of this paper for local practice?

Are the results of this study generalisable to your patients? (Does your patient resemble those in the study? What are your patient's preferences? Are there alternative treatments available?)

One-year follow-up of preventive intervention is important; the authors add that, in the present project, the intervention was provided through to grade 5 and that future results will examine the effects of multiple years of exposure.

No mention is made of teachers' views of the programme, nor of whether parents found change at home.

Additional comments

The authors note that the effects of the intervention with the non-high-risk children may depend on a simultaneous intervention with the high-risk children, as improved behaviour in the high-risk children may reduce teacher stress and may improve classroom peer relations among other children.

They also note that they cannot rule out the hypotheses that teachers who are better at implementing the universal model are just better teachers in general and that the general quality of the teaching may account for these effects.

appraisal of studies included in Barlow's (1999) systematic review

Table 1 Summary of the critical appraisal of included meta-analyses

Criteria for methodological adequacy	Cedar & Levant (1990)	Todres & Bunston (1993)	Serketich & Dumas (1996)
Validity			
Focused clinical question	+	+	+
Criteria for article inclusion	+	+	+
Relevant studies missed	−	−	−
Validity of included studies appraised	+	+	+
Assessments of studies reproducible	+	−	+
Results similar from study to study	−	−	−
Results			
Overall results	+	+	+
Precision of results	+	−	+
Application to other parents and children			
Application to parents and children	−	−	−
All clinically important outcomes	−	+	−
Benefits worth harm and costs	−	−	−

+ = Yes; − = Not satisfactory/don't know.

Table taken from Barlow (1999).

Table 2 Summary of critical appraisal of included studies[a]

Criteria for methodological adequacy	S94	S92	WS88	WS84	K77	F75	C95	M94	L92	S92	S87	D85	P81	F80	B80	F75
Validity																
Randomisation[b]	++	++	++	++	++	++	+	+	+	+	+	?	+	+	+	+
Attrition/drop-outs accounted for	+	+	+	+	–	+	+	+	–	–	+	+	–	–	+	–
Blinding to treatment[c]	n/a	n/a	+	+	+	n/a	–	n/a	n/a	–	–	n/a	+	–	+	n/a
Similarity of groups at start of trial	+	+	+	+	–	–	+	–	–	+	–	?	–	–	+	+
Equal treatment of groups	+	+	+	+	+	+	+	+	+	+	+	–	+	+	+	+
Results																
Overall results favoured parent-training																
using parenting reports	+	+	+	+	+	+	+	+	+	+	+	+	+	+	+	–
using independent observations	n/a	n/a	+	+	+	n/a	–	n/a	n/a	+	+	–	+	–	–	n/a
Precision of results	+	+	+	+	+	+	+	+	+	+	+	+	+	+	+	+
Applicability																
Generalisability[d]	+	+	+++	+++	+	+	+++	+	++	++	++	++	+	++	+	+

Column headings for references are, left to right: S94, Sheeber & Johnson (1994); S92, Spaccarelli et al (1992); WS88, Webster-Stratton et al (1988); WS84, Webster-Stratton (1984); K77, Karoly & Rosenthal (1977); F75, Freeman (1975); C95, Cunningham et al (1995); M94, Mullen et al (1994); L92, Lawes (1992); S92, Sutton (1992); S87, Scott & Stradling (1987); D85, Daly et al (1985); P81, Pinsker & Geoffroy (1981); F80, Firestone et al (1980); B80, Bernal et al (1980); F75, Frazier & Matthes (1975).

[a]This table does not include the two follow-up studies – Webster-Stratton et al (1989); Webster-Stratton (1990c).
[b] + = quasi-randomisation; ++ = strict randomisation.
[c]This refers to the blinding of independent assessors. n/a = 'not applicable', i.e. independent assessors were not used in the study.
[d] + = limited – volunteers/self-referral; ++ = included referred parents; +++ = children with clinical problems (i.e. children well above the mean using a standardised behaviour outcome measure).

Table taken from Barlow (1999).

questionnaire on parent-training programmes

	Y/N	Comments

1. Do you offer parent-training for children with conduct disorder, under 10 years old?

2. If No, is there a reason why not?

3. If you answered Yes to Q1, what types of programme do you offer, e.g. behavioural, group or individual?

4. Do you find these programmes effective?   Type 1
   Type 2

5. Have the programmes that you use been evaluated?

6. If Yes, what were the findings?

7. If No, do you have any plans to evaluate them   Type 1
   in the future?   Type 2

8. Which staff in your service carry out the parent-training?

9. Have the staff carrying out the training been trained specifically in techniques?

10. If Yes, where and by whom?

11. If No, would they like training?

12. Do you have plans to develop these programmes further?

13. Do you offer any of the following approaches   Family Therapy
    for young children with conduct disorder?   Behavioural Therapy
         Psychotherapy
         Other (please specify)

14. Approximately what percentage of referrals of children with conduct disorder come from:

    GPs?   %
    Paediatricians?   %
    Social Services?   %
    Education?   %
    Other (please specify)?   %

references

Achenbach, T. M. & Edelbrock, C. S. (1991) *Manual for the Child Behavior Checklist and Revised Child Behaviour Profile*. Burlington, VT: University Associates in Psychiatry.

Adler, A. (1927) *Understanding Human Nature*. New York: Greenberg.

— (1930) *The Education of Children*. New York: Greenberg.

American Academy of Child and Adolescent Psychiatry (1997) Practice parameters for the assessment and treatment of children and adolescents with conduct disorder. *Journal of the American Academy of Child and Adolescent Psychiatry*, **36**, Supplement.

American Psychiatric Association (2000) *Diagnostic and Statistical Manual of Mental Disorders* (4th edn, text revision) (DSM–IV). Washington, DC: American Psychiatric Association.

Appleton, P. L. & Hammond-Rowley, S. (2000) Addressing the population burden of child and adolescent mental health problems: a primary care model. *Child Psychology and Psychiatry Review*, **5**, 9–16.

Bandura, A. (1986) *Social Foundations of Thoughts and Action: A Social Cognitive Theory*. Englewood Cliffs, NJ: Prentice-Hall.

Bank, L., Hicks Marlowe, J., Reid, J. B., *et al* (1991) A comparative evaluation of parent-training interventions for families of chronic delinquents. *Journal of Abnormal Child Psychology*, **19**, 15–33.

Barclay, R. A. (1997) *Defiant Children: A Clinician's Manual for Assessment and Parent Training* (2nd edn). New York: Guilford Press.

Barlow, J. (1997) *Systematic Review of the Effectiveness of Parent-Training Programmes in Improving Behaviour Problems in Children Aged 3–10 Years*. Oxford: Department of Public Health, Health Services Research Unit.

— (1999) *Systematic Review of the Effectiveness of Parent-Training Programmes in Improving Behaviour Problems in Children Aged 3–10 Years* (2nd edn). Oxford: Department of Public Health, Health Services Research Unit.

— & Stewart-Brown, S. (2000) Behaviour problems and group-based parent education programs. *Journal of Developmental and Behavioural Pediatrics,* **21**, 356–370.

Barnett, W. S. (1993) Benefit–cost analysis of preschool education: findings from a 25-year follow-up. *American Journal of Orthopsychiatry*, **63**, 500–508.

Beck, C. T. (1998) The effects of postpartum depression on child development: a meta-analysis. *Archives of Psychiatric Nursing*, **12**, 12–20.

Bee, H. L., Barnard, K. E., Eyres, S. J., *et al* (1982) Prediction of IQ and language skill from peri-natal status, child performance, family characteristics, and mother–infant interaction. *Child Development*, **53**, 1134–1156.

Belsky, J. & MacKinnon, C. (1994) Transition to school: developmental trajectories and school experiences. *Early Education and Development*, **5**, 106–119.

Bernal, M. E., Klinnert, M. D. & Schultz, L. A. (1980) Outcome evaluation of behavioural parent-training and client-centred parent counselling for children with conduct-problems. *Journal of Applied Behavior Analysis*, **13**, 677–691.

Bordin, E. S. (1979) The generalisability of the psychoanalytic concept of the working alliance. *Psychotherapy, Theory Research and Practice*, **16**, 252–260.

Bowlby, J. (1969) *Attachment and Loss.* New York: Basic Books.

Brestan, E. V. & Eyberg, S. M. (1998) Effective psychosocial treatments of conduct disordered children and adolescents: 29 years, 82 studies and 5,272 kids. *Journal of Clinical Child Psychology*, **27**, 180–189.

Buchanan, A. (1999) *What Works for Troubled Children? Family Support for Children with Emotional and Behavioural Problems.* Ilford, Essex: Barnardo's.

Cantwell, D. P. & Baker, L. (1991) Association between attention deficit-hyperactivity disorder and learning disorders. *Journal of Learning Disabilities*, **24**, 88–95.

Carr, A. (1999) *The Hand Report of Child and Adolescent Clinical Psychology: A Contextual Approach.* London: Routledge.

Cedar, B. & Levant, R. F. (1990) A meta-analysis of the effects of parent-effectiveness training. *American Journal of Family Therapy*, **18**, 373–384.

Chambless, D. L., Sanderson, W. C., Shoham, V., *et al* (1996) An update on empirically validated therapies. *Clinical Psychologist*, **49**, 5–18.

Coffman, S., Levitt, M. J., Guacci, N., *et al* (1992) Temperament and interactive effects: mothers and infants in a teaching situation. *Issues in Comprehensive Nursing*, **10**, 141–145.

Cohen J. (1981) *Statistical Power Analysis for the Behavioral Sciences* (2nd edn). Hillsdale, NJ: Erlbaum.

Coie, J. D. & Dodge, K. A. (1998) Aggression and antisocial behaviour. In *Handbook of Child Psychology. Vol. 3: Social, Emotional, and Personality Development* (5th edn) (eds W. Damon & N. Eisenberg), pp. 779–862. New York: Wiley.

—, Watt, N. F., West, S. G., *et al* (1993) The science of prevention: a conceptual framework and some directions for a national research program. *American Psychologist*, **48**, 1013–1022.

Conduct Problems Prevention Research Group (1999*a*) Initial impact of the fast track prevention trial for conduct problems: I. The high-risk sample. *Journal of Consulting and Clinical Psychology*, **67**, 631–647.

— (1999*b*) Initial impact of the fast track prevention trial for conduct problems: II. Classroom effects. *Journal of Consulting and Clinical Psychology*, **67**, 648–657.

Conners, C. K. (1989) *Conners' Rating Scales Manual.* New York: Multi-Health Systems.

—, Sitarenios, G., Parker, J. D., *et al* (1998*a*) Revision and restandardization of the Conners' Parent Rating Scale (CPRS-R): factor structure, reliability, and criterion validity. *Journal of Abnormal Child Psychology*, **26**, 257–268.

—, —, —, *et al* (1998*b*) Revision and restandardization of the Conners' Teacher Rating Scale (CTRS-R): factor structure, reliability, and criterion validity. *Journal of Abnormal Child Psychology*, **26**, 279–291.

Cunningham, C. (1998) Child and parent training sessions led to improved child behaviour in child conduct disorder. *Evidence-Based Mental Health*, **1**, 11.

—, Bremner, R. & Boyle, M. (1995) Large group community-based parenting programs for families of pre-schoolers. *Journal of Child Psychology and Psychiatry and Allied Disciplines*, **36**, 1141–1159.

Dadds, M. R. & McHugh, T. A. (1992) Social support and treatment outcomes in behavioural family therapy for child conduct problems. *Journal of Consulting and Clinical Psychology*, **60**, 252–259.

Daly, R. M., Holland, C. J., Forrest, P. A., *et al* (1985) Temporal generalisation of treatment effects over a 3-year period for a parent-training program – directive parental-counselling (dpc). *Canadian Journal of Behavioural Science – Review*, **17**, 379–388.

Davis, H. & Spurr, P. (1998) Parent counselling: an evaluation of community CAMHS. *Journal of Child Psychology and Psychiatry*, **39**, 365–376.

Dinkmeyer, D. & McKay, G. (1976) *Systematic Training for Effective Parenting.* Circle Pines, MN: American Guidance Service.

Dishion, T. J. & Andrews, D. W. (1995) Preventing escalation in problem behaviours with high-risk young adolescents: immediate and 1-year outcomes. Special section: Prediction and prevention of child and adolescent antisocial behaviour. *Journal of Consulting and Clinical Psychology*, **63**, 538–548.

—, Patterson, G. R., Stoolmiller, M., *et al* (1991) Family, school and behavioural antecedents to early adolescent involvement with antisocial peers. *Developmental Psychology*, **27**, 172–180.

Dodge, K. A. & Price, J. M. (1994) On the relation between social information processing and socially competent behavior in early school-aged children. *Child Development*, **65**, 1385–1397.

— & Schwartz, D. (1997) Social information processing mechanisms in aggressive behaviour. In *Handbook of Antisocial Behavior* (eds D. M. Stoof, J. Brieling & J. D. Maser), pp. 171–180. New York: Wiley.

—, Pettit, G. S. & Bates, J. E. (1994) Socialisation mediators of the relation between socio-economic status and child conduct problems. *Child Development*, **65**, 649–665.

Dolan, L. J., Kellam, S. G., Brown, C. H., *et al* (1993) The short-impact of two classroom-based preventive interventions on aggressive and shy behaviours and poor achievement. *Journal of Applied Developmental Psychology*, **14**, 317–345.

Dreikurs, R. & Soltz, V. (1964) *Children: The Challenge.* New York: Hawthorn.

Dumas, J. E. (1984) Interactional correlates of treatment outcome in behavioural parent-training. *Journal of Consulting and Clinical Psychology*, **52**, 946–954.

— & Wahler, R. G. (1983) Predictors of treatment outcome in parent training: mother insularity and socio-economic disadvantage. *Behavioural Assessment*, **5**, 301–313.

Duncan, G., Brooks-Gunn, J. & Klebanov, P. (1994) Economic deprivation and early childhood development. *Child Development*, **65**, 296–318.

Earls, F., Reich, W., Jung, K. G., *et al* (1988) Psychopathology in children of alcoholic and antisocial parents. *Alcoholism: Clinical and Experimental Research*, **12**, 481–487.

Eaves, L. J., Silberg, J. L., Meyer, J. M., *et al* (1997) Genetics and developmental psychopathology: 2. The main effects of genes and environment on behavioral problems in the Virginia Twin Study of Adolescent Behavioral Development. *Journal of Child Psychology and Psychiatry*, **38**, 965–980.

Elliott, D. S. (1994) Serious violent offenders: onset, developmental course, and termination. The American Society of Criminology 1993 Presidential Address. *Criminology*, **32**, 1–21.

Erickson, M., Egeland, B. & Pianta, R. (1989) The effects of maltreatment on the development of young children. In *Child Maltreatment: Theory and Research on the Causes and Consequences of Child Abuse and Neglect* (eds D. Cicchetti & V. Carlson). New York: Cambridge University Press.

Evans, E. G. (1976) Behaviour problems in children. *Child Care and Health Development*, **2**, 35–43.

Eyberg, S. M. (1992) Parent and teacher behavior inventories for the assessment of conduct problem behaviors in children. In *Innovations in Clinical Practice: A Source Report, Vol. 11* (eds L. Vandecreek, S. Knapp & T. L. Jackson), pp. 261–270. Sarasota, FL: Professional Resource Press.

—, Boggs, S. & Algina, J. (1995) Parent–child interaction therapy: a psychosocial model for the treatment of young children with conduct problem behaviour and their families. *Psychopharmacology Bulletin*, **31**, 83–91.

Farrington, D. P. (1977) The effects of public labelling. *British Journal of Criminology*, **17**, 112–125.

— (1989) Early predictors of adolescent aggression and adult violence. *Violence and Victims*, **4**, 79–100.

— (1990) Implications of the criminal career research for the prevention of offending. *Journal of Adolescents*, **13**, 93–113.

— (1995) The development of offending and antisocial behaviour from childhood: key findings from the Cambridge Study in Delinquent Development. *Journal of Child Psychology and Psychiatry*, **36**, 929–964.

Fergusson, D. M. & Lynskey, M. T. (1995) Childhood circumstances, adolescent adjustment and suicide attempts in a New Zealand birth cohort. *Journal of the American Academy of Child and Adolescent Psychiatry*, **34**, 612–622.

Finkelhor, D. & Berliner, L. (1995) Research on the treatment of sexually abused children: a review and recommendations. *Journal of the American Academy of Child and Adolescent Psychiatry*, **34**, 1408–1423.

Firestone, P., Kelly, M. J. & Fike, S. (1980) Are fathers necessary in parent-training groups? *Journal of Clinical Child Psychology*, **9**, 44–47.

Forehand, R. & McMahon, R. J. (1981) *Helping the Noncompliant Child: A Clinician's Guide to Parent training*. New York: Guilford Press.

—, Middlebrook, J., Rogers, T., *et al* (1983) Dropping out of parent-training. *Behaviour Research and Therapy*, **21**, 663–668.

Frazier, F. & Matthes, W. A. (1975) Parent education: a comparison of adlerian and behavioural approaches. *Elementary School Guidance and Counseling*, **10**, 31–38.

Freedman, B. J., Rosenthal, L., Donahoe, C. P., *et al* (1978) A social-behavioral analysis of skill deficits in delinquent and nondelinquent adolescent boys. *Journal of Consulting and Clinical Psychology*, **46**, 1448–1462.

Freeman, C. (1975) Adlerian mother study groups and traditional mother discussion groups: affects on attitudes and behavior. *Journal of Individual Psychology*, **31**, 37–50.

Frick, P. J., Kamphaus, R. W., Lahey, B. B., *et al* (1991) Academic underachievement and the disruptive behavior disorders. *Journal of Consulting and Clinical Psychology*, **59**, 289–294.

Frost, N., Johnson L., Stein, M., *et al* (1997) *Negotiated Friendships: Home-Start and the Delivery of Family Support*. Leicester: Home-Start UK.

Goodman, R. & Stevenson, J. (1989) A twin study of hyperactivity: II. The aetiological role of genes, family relationships and perinatal adversity. *Journal of Child Psychology and Psychiatry*, **30**, 691–709.

Goodman, S. H. & Brumley, H. E. (1990) Schizophrenic and depressed mothers: relational deficits in parenting. *Developmental Psychology*, **26**, 31–39.

Gordon, T. (1975) *Parent Effectiveness Training*. New York: Peter Wyden.

Graham, F. P. & Rutter, M. (1973) Psychiatric disorders in young adolescents. *Proceedings of the Royal Society of Medicine*, **66**, 1226–1229.

Graham, P. (1991) *Child Psychiatry: A Developmental Approach* (2nd edn). Oxford: Oxford University Press.

Greenberg, M. T. & Kusche, C. A. (1993) *Promoting Social and Emotional Development in Deaf Children: The PATHS Project*. Seattle: University of Washington Press.

— & — (1998) Preventive intervention for school-aged deaf children: the PATHS curriculum. *Journal of Deaf Studies and Deaf Education*, **3**, 49–63.

— & Speltz, M. (1988) Attachment and the ontogeny of conduct problems. In *Clinical Implications of Attachment* (eds J. Belsky & T. Nezworski), pp. 177–218. Hillsdale, NJ: Erlbaum.

— & Speltz, M. L. (1993) The role of attachment in the early development of disruptive behaviour problems. *Development and Psychopathology*, **5**, 191–213.

—, Kusche, C. A., Cook, E. T., *et al* (1995) Promoting emotional competence in school-aged children: the effects of the PATHS curriculum. *Development and Psychopathology*, **7**, 117–136.

Hall, L. A., Gurley, D. N., Sachs, B., *et al* (1991) Psychosocial predictors of maternal depressive symptoms, parenting attitudes, and child behaviour in single parent families. *Nursing Research*, **40**, 214–220.

Hamilton, S. B. & MacQuiddy, S. L. (1984) Self-administered behavioural parent training: enhancement of treatment efficacy using a time-out signal seat. *Journal of Clinical Child Psychology*, **13**, 61–69.

Hanf (1969) A two stage program for modifying maternal controlling during the mother–child interaction. Paper presented at the meeting of the Western Psychological Association, Vancouver, British Columbia, Canada. (Cited in McMahon, 1994.)

Hausman, B. & Hammen, C. (1993) Parenting in homeless families: the double crisis. *American Journal of Orthopsychiatry*, **63**, 358–369.

Hawkins, J. D., Catalano, R. F., Morrison, D. M., *et al* (1992) The Seattle Social Development Project: effects of the first four years on protective factors and problem behaviors. In *Preventing Antisocial Behaviour: Interventions from Birth to Adolescence* (eds J. McCord & R. E. Tremblay), pp. 139–161. New York: Guilford Press.

Hinshaw, S. P. (1992) Externalising behavior problems and academic underachievement in childhood and adolescence: causal relationships and underlying mechanisms. *Psychological Bulletin*, **111**, 127–155.

Holden, G. W., Lavigne, V. V. & Cameron, A. M. (1990) Probing the continuum of effectiveness in parent training: characteristics of parents and preschoolers. *Journal of Clinical Child Psychology*, **19**, 2–8.

Home Office (1998) *Supporting Families – A Consultation Document*. London: Home Office.

Horvath, A. O. (1994) Research on the alliance. In *The Working Alliance: Theory, Research and Practice* (eds A. O. Horvath & L. S. Greenberg), pp. 259–280. New York: Wiley.

House of Commons Health Committee (1997) *Child and Adolescent Mental Health Services. Health Committee Fourth Report: Session 1996–97, HC26–I*. London: House of Commons.

Johnson, C. A. & Katz, R. C. (1973) Using parents as change agents for their children: a review. *Journal of Child Psychology and Psychiatry and Allied Disciplines*, **14**, 181–200.

Johnson, D. (1990) The Houston Parent–Child Development Center Project: disseminating a viable program for enhancing at-risk families. *Prevention in Human Service*, **7**, 89–108.

Karoly, P. & Rosenthal, M. (1977) Training parents in behaviour modification: effects on perceptions of family interaction and deviant child behaviour. *Behaviour Therapy*, **8**, 406–410.

Kazdin, A. E. (1987) Treatment of antisocial behaviour in children: current status and future directions. *Psychological Bulletin*, **102**, 187–203.

— (1990) Premature termination from treatment among children referred for antisocial behaviour. *Journal of Child Psychology and Psychiatry and Allied Disciplines*, **31**, 415–425.

— (1993) Treatment of conduct disorder: progress and directions in psychotherapy research. *Developmental Psychology*, **5**, 277–310.

— (1995) *Conduct Disorders in Childhood and Adolescence.* Thousand Oaks, CA: Sage.

— (1996) Problem solving and parent management in treating aggressive and antisocial behavior. In *Psychosocial Treatments for Child and Adolescent Disorders: Empirically Based Strategies for Clinical Practice* (eds E. D. Hibbs & P. S. Jensen), pp. 377–408. Washington, DC: American Psychological Association.

Knapp, M., Scott, S. & Davies, J. (1999) The cost of antisocial behaviour in younger children: a pilot study of economic and family impact. *Clinical Child Psychology and Psychiatry*, **4**, 457–473.

Kusche, C. A. & Greenberg, M. T. (1994) *The PATHS Curriculum.* Seattle, WA: Development Research and Programs.

Lawes, G. (1992) Individual parent-training implemented by nursery nurses: evaluation of a program for mothers of pre-school children. *Behavioural Psychotherapy*, **20**, 239–256.

Lloyd, E. (ed.) (1999) *Parenting Matters: What Works in Parenting Education?* Ilford, Essex: Barnardo's.

Loeber, R. (1982) The stability of antisocial and delinquent child behaviour: a review. *Child Development*, **53**, 1431–1446.

— (1990) Development and risk factors of juvenile antisocial behaviour and delinquency. *Clinical Psychology Review*, **10**, 1–41.

— & Dishion, T. J. (1983) Early predictors of male delinquency: a review. *Psychological Bulletin*, **94**, 69–99.

—, Wung, P., Keenan, K., *et al* (1993) Developmental pathways in disruptive child behaviour. *Developmental Psychopathology*, **5**, 101–131.

Long, P., Forehand, R., Wierson, M., *et al* (1994) Does parent training with young noncompliant children have long-term effects? *Behaviour Research and Therapy*, **32**, 101–107.

Luntz, B. K. & Widom, C. S. (1994) Antisocial personality disorder in abused and neglected children. *American Journal of Psychiatry*, **151**, 670–674.

Lyons-Ruth, K. (1996) Attachment relationships among children with aggressive behaviour problems: the role of disorganised early attachment patterns. *Journal of Consulting and Clinical Psychology*, **64**, 64–73.

Marshall, J. & Watt, P. (1999) *Child Behaviour Problems: A Literature Review of the Size and Nature of the Problem and Prevention Interventions in Childhood.* Perth, Western Australia: Interagency Committee on Children's Futures.

Maughan, B. & Rutter, M. (1998) Continuities and discontinuities in antisocial behavior from childhood to adult life. *Advances in Clinical Child Psychology*, **20**, 1–47.

McLoyd, V. C. (1990) The impact of economic hardship on black families and children: psychological distress, parenting and socio-emotional development. *Child Development*, **61**, 311–346.

McMahon, R. J. (1994) Diagnosis, assessment and treatment of externalising problems in children: the role of longitudinal data. *Journal of Consulting and Clinical Psychology*, **62**, 901–917.

McNeil, C. B., Eyberg, S., Eisenstadt, T. H., *et al* (1991) Parent–child interaction therapy with behaviour problem children: generalisation of treatment effects to the school setting. *Journal of Clinical Child Psychology*, **20**, 140–151.

Mednick, S. A. & Kandel, E. S. (1988) Congenital determinants of violence. *Bulletin of the American Academy of Psychiatric Law*, **16**, 101–109.

Meltzer, H., Gatwood, R., Goodman, R., *et al* (2000) *Mental Health of Children and Adolescents in Great Britain.* London: The Stationery Office.

Mental Health Foundation (1999) *Bright Futures: Promoting Children and Young People's Mental Health.* London: Mental Health Foundation.

Miller, D. & Jang, M. (1977) Children of alcoholics: a 20-year longitudinal study. *Social Work Research and Abstracts*, **13**, 23–29.

Moffit, T., Caspi, A. & Dickson, N. (1996) Childhood onset versus adolescent onset. *Developmental Psychology*, **8**, 399–424.

Mullen, E., Quigley, K. & Glanville, B. (1994) A controlled evaluation of the impact of a parent-training programme on child behaviour and mothers' general well-being. *Counselling Psychology Quarterly*, **7**, 167–179.

National Assembly for Wales (2000) *Child and Adolescent Mental Health Services. Everybody's Business; Consultation Strategy.* Cardiff: National Assembly for Wales.

NHS Central Research and Development Committee (1995) *Improving the Health of Mothers and Children: NHS Priorities for Research and Development.* London: Department of Health.

NHS Centre for Reviews and Dissemination (1997) Mental health promotion in high risk groups. *Effective Health Care Bulletin*, **3**, 3–12.

Normand, C. L., Zoccolillo, M., Tremblay, R. E., *et al* (1996) In the beginning: looking for the roots of babies' difficult temperament. In *Growing Up in Canada: National Longitudinal Survey of Children and Youth*, pp.55–68. Ottawa: Statistics Canada.

Offord, D. R., Boyle, M. H. & Flemming, J. E. (1989) Ontario Child Health Study: summary of selected results. *Canadian Journal of Psychiatry*, **34**, 483–491.

—, Kraemer, H. C., Kazdin, A. E., *et al* (1998) Lowering the burden of suffering from child psychiatric disorder: trade-offs among clinical, targeted, and universal interventions. *Journal of the American Academy of Child and Adolescent Psychiatry*, **37**, 686–694.

Orrell-Valente, J. K., Pinderhughes, E. E., Valente Jr, E., *et al* (1999) If it's offered will they come? Influences on parents' participation in a community-based conduct problems prevention program. *American Journal of Community Psychology*, **27**, 753–783.

Patterson, G. R. (1982) *Coercive Family Process.* Eugene, OR: Castalia.

— (1986) Performance models for antisocial boys. *American Psychologist*, **41**, 432–444.

— & Chamberlain, P. (1988) Treatment process: a problem at three levels. In *The State of the Art in Family Therapy Research: Controversies and Recommendations* (ed. L. Wynne), pp. 189–223. New York: Family Process Press.

— & — (1994) A functional analysis of resistance during parent training therapy. *Clinical Psychology: Science and Practice*, **1**, 53–70.

— & Forgatch, M. S. (1995) Predicting future clinical adjustment from treatment outcomes and process variables. *Psychological Assessment*, **7**, 275–285.

— & Guillion, M. E. (1968) *Living with Children: New Methods for Parents and Teachers.* Champaign, IL: Research Press.

—, DeBaryshe, B. D. & Ramsey, E. (1989) A development perspective on antisocial behaviour. *The American Psychologist*, **44**, 329–335.

Peed, S., Roberts, M. & Forehand, R. (1977) Evaluation of the effectiveness of a standardized parent training program in altering the interaction of mothers and their non-compliant children. *Behavior Modification*, **1**, 323–350.

PEEP (1998) *PEEP Annual Report 1997–1998.* Oxford: PEEP Centre.

Perry, D. G., Perry, L. C. & Rasmussen, P. (1986) Cognitive social learning mediators of aggression. *Child Development*, **57**, 700–711.

Pinsker, M. & Geoffroy, K. (1981) A comparison of parent-effectiveness training and behaviour modification parent-training. *Family Relations*, **30**, 61–68.

Plomin, R. (1994) The Emanuel Miller Memorial Lecture 1993. Genetic research and identification of environmental influences. *Journal of Child Psychology and Psychiatry*, **35**, 817–834.

Prinz, R. J. & Miller, G. E. (1996) Parental engagement in interventions for children at risk for conduct disorder. In *Preventing Childhood Disorders, Substance Abuse, and Delinquency* (eds R. DeV. Peters & R. J. McMahon), pp. 161–183. Thousand Oaks, CA: Sage.

Prior, M., Smart, D., Sanson, A., *et al* (1993) Sex differences in psychological adjustment from infancy to 8 years. *Journal of the American Academy of Child and Adolescent Psychiatry*, **32**, 291–305.

Provence, S. & Naylor, A. (1983) *Working with Disadvantaged Parents and Children: Scientific Issues and Practice.* New Haven, CT: Yale University Press.

Puckering, C., Rogers, J., Mills, M., *et al* (1994) Process and evaluation of a group intervention for mothers with parenting difficulties. *Child Abuse Review*, **3**, 299–310.

Pugh, G., De'Ath, E. & Smith, C. (1994) *Confident Parents, Confident Children: Policy and Practice in Parent Education and Support.* London: National Children's Bureau.

Raine, A., Brennan, P. & Mednick, S. A. (1994) Birth complications combined with early maternal rejection at 1 year predispose to violent crime at age 18 years. *Archives of General Psychiatry*, **51**, 984–988.

Reid, J. B. (1993) Prevention of conduct disorder before and after school entry: relating interventions to developmental findings. *Developmental Psychopathology*, **5**, 243–262.

—, Eddy, J. M., Fetrow, R. A., *et al* (1999) Description and immediate impacts of a preventative intervention for conduct disorder. *American Journal of Community Psychology*, **27**, 483–517.

Richman, N., Stevenson, J. & Graham P. J. (1982) *Preschool to School: Behavioural Study.* London: Academic Press.

Robins, L. N. (1966) *Deviant Children Grown Up: A Sociological and Psychiatric Study of Sociopathic Personality.* Baltimore, MD: Williams & Wilkins.

— (1978) Sturdy childhood predictors of adult antisocial behaviour: replications from longitudinal studies. *Psychological Medicine*, **8**, 611–622.

— (1991) Conduct disorder. *Journal of Child Psychology and Psychiatry*, **32**, 193–212.

Rogers, C. (1951) *Client-Centred Therapy.* Boston, MA: Houghton-Mifflin.

Rutter, M. (1979) Protective factors in children's response to stress and disadvantage. In *Primary Prevention of Disadvantage, Vol. 3* (eds W. M. Ken & J. E. Rolf), pp. 49–74. Hanover, NH: University Press of New England.

— (1985) Resilience in the face of adversity: protective factors and resistance to psychiatric disorder. *British Journal of Psychiatry*, **147**, 598–611.

— (1988) *Studies of Psychological Risk: The Power of Longitudinal Data.* New York: Cambridge University Press.

— & Giller, H. (1983) *Juvenile Delinquency Trends and Perspectives.* New York: Penguin Books.

—, Tizard, J. & Whitmore, K. (1970) *Education, Health, and Behaviour.* London: Longmore.

—, Cox, A., Tupling, C., et al (1975) Attainment and adjustment in two geographical areas. *British Journal of Psychiatry*, **126**, 493–509.

—, Tizard, J., Yule, W., et al (1976) Isle of Wight studies, 1964–1974. *Psychological Medicine*, **6**, 313–332.

—, Giller, H. & Hagler, A. (1998) *Antisocial Behaviour by Young People*. New York: Cambridge University Press.

Rydelius, P. A. (1988) The development of antisocial behaviour and sudden violent death. *Acta Psychiatrica Scandinavica*, **77**, 398–403.

Sanders, M. R. & Markie-Dadds, C. L. (1996) Triple P: a multilevel family intervention program for children with disruptive behaviour disorders. In *Early Intervention and Prevention in Mental Health Applications of Clinical Psychology* (eds P. Cotton & H. Jackson), pp. 59–87. Melbourne: Australian Psychology Society.

—, —, Tully, L. A., et al (2000) The Triple P–Positive Parenting Program: a comparison of enhanced, standard, and self-directed behavioural family intervention for parents of children with early onset conduct problems. *Journal of Consulting and Clinical Psychology*, **68**, 624–640.

Schweinhart, L. J. & Weikart, D. P. (1997) The High/Scope Preschool Curriculum Comparison Study through age 23. *Early Childhood Research*, **12**, 117–143.

Scott, M. J. & Stradling, S. G. (1987) Evaluation of a group program for parents of problem children. *Behavioural Psychotherapy*, **15**, 224–239.

Scott, S. (1995) Disobedient and aggressive children. Part 2: management. *Maternal and Child Health*, February, 44–50.

— (1998) Aggressive behaviour in childhood. *British Medical Journal*, **316**, 202–206.

— & Sylva, K. (1997) Enabling parents, supporting parents, parenting children with challenging behaviour. *Department of Health Research Initiative Newsletter*, **2**, 4–5.

Seitz, V., Rosenbaum, L. K. & Apfel, N. H. (1985) Effects of family support intervention: a ten-year follow-up. *Child Development*, **56**, 376–391.

Serketich, W. J. & Dumas, J. E. (1996) The effectiveness of behavioural parent-training to modify antisocial behaviour in children: a meta-analysis. *Behaviour Therapy*, **27**, 171–186.

Shaw, D. S. & Winslow, E. B. (1997) Precursors and correlates of antisocial behavior from infancy to preschool. In *Handbook of Antisocial Behavior* (eds D. M. Stoff, J. Breiling & J. D. Maser), pp. 148–158. New York: Wiley.

Sheeber, L. B. & Johnson, J. H. (1994) Evaluation of a temperament-focused parent-training programme. *Journal of Clinical Child Psychology*, **23**, 249–259.

Silberg, J., Rutter, M., Meyer, J., et al (1996) Genetic and environmental influences on the covariation between hyperactivity and conduct disturbance in juvenile twins. *Journal of Child Psychology and Psychiatry and Allied Disciplines*, **37**, 803–816.

Skinner, B. F. (1953) *Science and Human Behavior*. New York: Macmillan.

Smith, C. (1996) *Developing Parenting Programmes*. London: National Children's Bureau.

Spaccarelli, S., Cotler, S. & Penman, D. (1992) Problem-solving skills training as a supplement to parent-training. *Cognitive Therapy and Research*, **16**, 1–18.

Spender, Q. & Scott, S. (1997) Management of antisocial behaviour in childhood. *Advances in Psychiatric Treatment*, **3**, 128–137.

Stein, A., Gath, D. H., Bucher, J., et al (1991) The relationship between post-natal depression and mother–child interaction. *British Journal of Psychiatry*, **158**, 46–52.

Sutton,C. (1992) Training parents to manage difficult children: a comparison of methods. *Behavioural Psychology*, **9**, 115–139.

Task Force on Promotion and Dissemination of Psychological Procedures (1995) Training in and dissemination of empirically-validated psychological treatments: Report and recommendations. *Clinical Psychologist*, **48**, 3–23.

Taylor, T. K. & Biglan, A. (1998) Behavioral family interventions for improving child-rearing: a review of the literature for clinicians and policy makers. *Clinical Child and Family Psychology Review*, **1**, 41–60.

—, Schmidt, F., Pepler, D., *et al* (1998) A comparison of eclectic treatment with Webster-Stratton's Parents and Children Series in a children's mental health center: a randomized control trial. *Behaviour Therapy*, **29**, 221–240.

Thapar, A., Hervas, A. & McGuffin, P. (1995) Childhood hyperactivity scores are highly heritable and show sibling competition effects: twin study evidence. *Behavior Genetics*, **25**, 537–544.

Todres, R. & Bunston, T. (1993) Parent-education programme evaluation: a review of the literature. *Canadian Journal of Community Mental Health*, **12**, 225–257.

Tremblay, R. E., Vitaro, F., Bertrand, L., *et al* (1992) Parent and child training to prevent early onset of delinquency: the Montreal Longitudinal–Experimental Study. In *Preventing Antisocial Behaviour: Interventions From Birth Through Adolescence* (eds J. McCord & R. E. Tremblay), pp. 117–138. New York: Guilford Press.

—, Pagani-Kurtz, L., Masse, L. C., *et al* (1995) A bimodal preventive intervention for disruptive kindergarten boys: its impact through mid-adolescence. *Journal of Consulting and Clinical Psychology*, **63**, 560–568.

Underwood, M. K. (1997) Peer social status and children's understanding of the expression and control of positive and negative emotions. *Merrill-Palmer Quarterly*, **43**, 610–634.

Walters, G. D. (1992) A meta-analysis of the gene–crime relationship. *Criminology*, **30**, 595–613.

Webster-Stratton, C. (1984) Randomized trial of two parent-training programs for families with conduct-disordered children. *Journal of Consulting and Clinical Psychology*, **52**, 666–678.

— (1989) Systematic comparison of consumer satisfaction of three cost-effective parent-training programs for conduct problem children. *Behaviour Therapy*, **20**, 103–115.

— (1990*a*) Stress: a potential disruptor of parent perceptions and family interactions. *Journal of Clinical Child Psychology* (Special issue: the stresses of parenting), **19**, 302–312.

— (1990*b*) Enhancing the effectiveness of self-administered videotape parent-training for families with conduct-problem children. *Journal of Abnormal Child Psychology*, **18**, 479–492.

— (1990*c*) Long-term follow-up of families with young conduct-problem children: from pre-school to grade school. *Journal of Clinical Child Psychology*, **19**, 144–149.

— (1993) Strategies for helping early school-aged children with oppositional defiant and conduct disorders: the importance of home–school partnerships. *School Psychology Review*, **22**, 437–457.

— (1994) Advancing videotape parent-training. *Journal of Consulting and Clinical Psychology*, **62**, 583–593.

— (1996) Early intervention with videotape modeling: programs for families of children with oppositional defiant disorder or conduct disorder. In *Psychosocial Treatments for Child and Adolescent Disorders: Empirically Based Strategies for Clinical Practice* (eds E. D. Hibbs & P. S. Jensen), pp. 377–408. Washington, DC: American Psychological Association.

— (1997) From parent training to community building. Families in society. *Journal of Contemporary Human Services*, **78**, 156–171.

— (1998) Preventing conduct problems in Head Start children. *Journal of Consulting and Clinical Psychology*, **66**, 715–730.

— & Hammond, M. (1990) Predictors of treatment outcome in parent-training for families with conduct-problem children. *Behaviour Therapy*, **21**, 319–337.

— & — (1997) Treating children with early onset conduct disorder. *Journal of Consulting and Clinical Psychology*, **65**, 93–109.

— & — (1999) Marital conflict management skills, parenting style, and early-onset conduct problems: processes and pathways. *Journal of Child Psychology and Psychiatry*, **40**, 917–927.

— & Herbert, M. (1993) What really happens in parent-training? *Behaviour Modification*, **17**, 407–456.

— &— (1994) *Troubled Families, Problem Children. Working With Parents: A Collaborative Process.* New York: Wiley.

— & Spitzer, A. (1991) Development, reliability and validity of a parent daily telephone discipline interview: DDI. *Behavioural Assessment*, **13**, 221–239.

—, Kolpacoff, M. & Hollinsworth, T. (1988) Self-administered videotape therapy for families with conduct-problem children: comparison with two cost-effective treatments and a control group. *Journal of Consulting and Clinical Psychology*, **56**, 558–566.

—, Hollinsworth, T. & Kolpacoff, M. (1989) The long-term effectiveness and clinical significance of three cost-effective training programs for families with conduct-problem children. *Journal of Consulting and Clinical Psychology*, **57**, 550–553.

Weisz, J. R., Weiss, B., Han, S. S., *et al* (1995) Effects of psychotherapy with children and adolescents revisited: a meta-analysis of treatment outcome studies. *Psychological Bulletin*, **117**, 450–468.

Wells, K. C. & Egan, J. (1988) Social learning and systems family therapy for childhood oppositional disorder: comparative treatment outcome. *Comprehensive Psychiatry*, **29**, 138–146.

Werner, E. E. (1992) The children of Kauai: resiliency and recovery in adolescence and adulthood. *Journal of Adolescent Health*, **13**, 262–268.

— (1994) Overcoming the odds. *Journal of Developmental Behavioral Pediatrics*, **15**, 131–136.

West, O. J. & Farrington, D. P. (1973) *The Delinquent Way of Life.* London: Heinemann.

White, S. H. (1965) Evidence for a hierarchal arrangement of learning processes. In *Advances in Child Development and Behaviour, Vol. 2* (eds L. P. Lipsett & C. C. Spiker), pp. 41–89. New York: Academic Press.

Wilson, J. Q. & Herrnstein, R. (1985) *Crime and Human Nature.* New York: Simon & Schuster.

Wootton, J. M., Frick, P. J., Shelton, K. K., *et al* (1997) Ineffective parenting and childhood conduct problems: the moderating role of callous-unemotional traits. *Journal of Consulting and Clinical Psychology*, **65**, 301–308.

World Health Organization (1992) *The ICD–10 Classification of Mental and Behavioural Disorders: Clinical Descriptions and Diagnostic Guidelines.* Geneva: World Health Organization.

Yoshikawa, H. (1994) Prevention as cumulative protection: effects of early family support and education on chronic delinquency and its risks. *Psychological Bulletin*, **115**, 28–54.

Zangwill, W. M. (1983) An evaluation of a parent training program. *Child and Family Behaviour Therapy*, **5**, 1–6.

Zigler, E., Taussig, C. & Black, K. (1992) Early childhood intervention: a promising preventative for juvenile delinquency. *American Psychologist*, **47**, 997–1006.

—, Piorkowski, C. S. & Collins, R. (1994) Health services in Head Start. *Annual Review of Public Health*, **15**, 511–534.

index